LOSS PREVENTION

in the Retail Business

LOSS PREVENTION

in the Retail Business

RUDOLPH C. KIMIECIK
CHRIS THOMAS

WILEY

JOHN WILEY & SONS, INC.

For general information on our other products and services or for technical support, please contact our Customer Care Department within the United States at (800) 762-2974, outside the United States at (317) 572-3993 or fax (317) 572-4002.

Wiley also publishes its books in a variety of electronic formats. Some content that appears in print may not be available in electronic books. For more information about Wiley products, visit our web site at www.wiley.com.

Library of Congress Cataloging-in-Publication Data:

Kimiecik, Rudolph C.
   Loss prevention in the retail business / Rudolph C. Kimiecik, Chris Thomas.
      p.   cm.
   Includes index.
   ISBN-13: 978-0-471-72321-9 (pbk.)
   ISBN-10: 0-471-72321-5 (pbk.)
   1. Retail trade—Security measures.   2. Business losses—Prevention.
3. Shoplifting—Prevention.   4. Employee theft—Prevention.   5. Fraud—Prevention.
I. Thomas, Chris.   II. Title.
   HF5429.27.K55   2006
   658.4'73—dc22
                                                                2005019999

Printed in the United States of America

10 9 8 7 6 5 4 3 2 1

CONTENTS

CHAPTER **3**

ALARM SYSTEMS AND OTHER PHYSICAL SECURITY MEASURES 47

CHAPTER **4**

SHOPLIFTING 63

PREFACE

I will never forget the day I got robbed. Although the robber did not hurt me and escaped with only the few dollars that were in my purse, I have played out the scene a hundred times in my head, envisioning a different outcome. If I noticed that he was wearing a motorcycle helmet—and I was also observant enough to think, *But where's his motorcycle?* as I approached the building—I wonder today, why did I continue on my path? I could easily have stayed in my car with the doors locked. I could have stared at him, sizing him up to let him know I had clearly seen him. I could have just driven away.

Instead, I thought, *Hmm, that's odd*, went about my business, and turned my back on him for a split second—only to have him bound over a small hedge and poke something in my side. A gun? A knife? I was too afraid to look. He told me not to move, and I froze. I was lucky, I guess, that he grabbed the purse and ran; luckier still that my car keys fell out of it as he made his getaway.

As a prospective or current retail store owner or manager, the best crime-fighting advice you can be given is to always, *always* be observant and alert. But the second piece of advice that should accompany it is "Then, act on what you see." If something doesn't look or feel "right," it's probably not. Act accordingly.

Reading this book is an excellent first step for retail management students, because it will hone your sense of observation and alert you to a few of the many ways people can rob you, by stealing from your business. Employees, customers, suppliers, distributors, accountants—almost no one is immune to temptation under certain circumstances. And retailers today don't have to be paranoid to be appropriately cautious.

The information in the book is based on a series of seminars given by coauthor Rudolph C. Kimiecik, a retail security and loss prevention specialist with more than 35 years of professional experience. It covers a wide range of critical loss prevention subjects, which we have tailored specifically to the retail trade. It is organized into the following 10 umbrella topics:

Personal safety (Chapter 1) should be the top priority of any loss prevention program, because merchandise can be replaced but a human life cannot. This chapter delves into situations other than robberies and burglaries, too, with the addition of civil unrest and weather-related precautions, plus tips for safer daily functions such as opening and closing the store and making bank deposits.

Physical security (Chapter 2) involves the means criminals use to break into stores. We cover the precautions for doors and windows, roofs, walls, and ductwork, and also how to keep track of building and department keys on an ongoing basis. The discussion continues in Chapter 3, with basic information about alarms, lighting, and closed-circuit television monitoring.

Chapters 4, 5, and 6 explain the who, what, and how of three types of crime that hit the retail industry the hardest: shoplifting, armed robbery, and fraud. The latter includes everything from check and credit card scams to counterfeit bills and con artists, with plenty of suggestions for preventing problems. We also provide some commonsense ground rules for apprehending and prosecuting thieves.

Chapters 7 and 8 take the fraud discussion several steps further, into territory that some retailers find most uncomfortable—the dual emotional and financial hits they take when thieves are either employees or vendors. The fact is that more than half of all retail thefts are committed by these supposedly trusted sources, and merchants must be scrupulous in setting policies and procedures, and vigilant in enforcing them. As Chapter 8 points out, theft can occur anywhere in the supply chain, from dishonest distributors, to warehouse workers in collusion with bookkeepers, to delivery drivers for other companies.

Hiring trustworthy employees is the more optimistic topic of Chapter 9. Even so, we caution retailers to spend ample time prescreening all job applicants and double-checking the information they provide, keeping in mind the privacy and equal employment opportunity laws.

Chapter 10 rounds out the book with a rundown of the latest technology to accomplish many of the tasks in a good overall crime prevention program and outlines manageable steps to create and/or update such a program.

Although this book is written primarily as a guide for small and medium-size retailers who do not have their own corporate security staffs, the book can also be extremely useful for large, multiunit retailers who wish to enhance and supplement their existing loss prevention practices.

With the help of fellow writer Robin Heid of Perris, California, we've tried to pack as much information as possible into an informal, easy-to-understand format. A final—and we believe an important—note: The information presented is unbiased. None of us has a financial interest in, or hidden ties to, any alarm company, locksmith, safe manufacturer, or any other type of security service provider. Our information is gleaned from a wide variety of resources, as well as our own experiences, both good and bad.

Best of luck in creating a safe, inviting environment for your honest and loyal customers and employees.

Chris Thomas

PERSONAL
SAFETY

The personal safety of you and your employees is, by any realistic measure, the most important concern of a retail merchant—because it is a far greater risk than the store losing either cash or merchandise. Small retailers are especially at risk and must safeguard against burglary, robbery, and other crimes that potentially endanger the lives of store personnel.

In this chapter, you will learn about some key policies and practices that will help you to establish and maintain a high level of physical security for you and your employees, including:

- Store opening and closing procedures
- After-hours precautions
- Bank deposit safeguards
- Natural disaster and/or civil unrest procedures
- Bomb threat guidelines
- Emergency kits

OPENING AND CLOSING PROCEDURES

When it comes to armed robbery or serious bodily harm, the most vulnerable time for a store owner or manager is the half hour or so when they are in either opening or closing their stores. Criminals know the store is least likely to be busy during these times, and in the case of closing, the day's cash is often taken to the bank to be deposited after hours. The following paragraphs offer some general guidelines for extra vigilance during these time periods:

- **Never open the store alone.** The problem with any job is that it becomes rote after a while—and opening a store each and every business day is no exception. The smart store owner or manager comes to work fully alert and well aware of what's going on around him or her. As you approach the store and before getting out of your car, look carefully at the surroundings. Better yet, drive around the back of the store first, if possible. Look at the doors, windows, and walls for signs of forced entry. If you see ladders sitting in an alleyway, or if there are ropes dangling from the roof, these are clues that burglars may still be inside the store. If you're suspicious about anything, call the police.

   Make arrangements with your early-arriving employees to ensure that someone remains in position to go for help if you are held up while opening the store. If you must open with only one other employee present, make sure that employee does not immediately come into the store with you. Instead, the employee should remain outside the store until you give an "all clear" signal. If someone is hiding in the store and waiting for you, the employee posted outside will then be able to call the police if you do not return to the front of the store and give the prearranged "all clear" signal within a certain specified period of time.

- **If you have no alternative and must open by yourself, make every effort to have someone check on your safety.** Work out reciprocal arrangements with neighboring store owners to signal or call each other at designated times. If you are in an isolated area and there is no one else around, set up a procedure with your spouse or a friend to call you at a certain time (if you have not already called them). Tell the person to ask the police to check on you if you don't answer the phone.

Always lock the front door after you enter, and keep it locked (except to admit employees) until it is time to open for your normal business hours. Check for signs of a burglary. Be careful; the burglar could still be in the store. If you notice obvious signs that a burglary has been committed or see things that look suspicious, get out of the store immediately, relock the door, and call the police. Let them check the entire premises before you reenter.

- **Take extra precautions at closing time.** If you are not taking the day's proceeds with you for a bank deposit, lock all store funds in a safe. Do not leave any money in office drawers or in point-of-sale (POS) terminals (cash registers). Cash drawers should be left open to preclude thieves from breaking them apart to look for money. Lock all rear, side, or other auxiliary doors, windows, and other openings.

- **Make a complete area-by-area check for "*hide-ins*."** Some thieves hide in a store at closing time, then break out later with merchandise, usually leaving the scene with the aid of an accomplice. Others stay in a store all night to surprise and hold up the unsuspecting store owner whom they have observed opening alone. Pay particular attention, during your area check, to restrooms (including opening the doors to the stalls), back hallways, trash rooms, boiler rooms, basements, and areas under stairs and conveyor belts.

- **Leave some lights on in the store.** A well-lit storefront area, even when the store is closed, helps police, security guards, and other passersby to see any movement inside the store. Pay particular attention to lights in the office, the area around the safe, and departments containing high-value merchandise. Just prior to leaving:

  ◇ Test and set the burglar alarm system.
  ◇ If you have surveillance cameras, be sure they are operating and have a tape in the recording device.
  ◇ If you have a time lock that records unauthorized reentries into the store, be sure it is on and set.
  ◇ Lock the door.

  Before this ritual, of course, check for suspicious persons or activity in the area. If something doesn't seem right to you, do not hesitate to call the police.

- **Never close the store alone, and never remain in the store alone after closing hours.** This is of utmost importance. Try to keep as many employees with you as possible. It is strongly recommended that, shortly before you close, you have an employee leave the store and watch the entire closing procedure from a discreet distance and remain posted there until you lock up and safely leave the area. This employee should have a cellular phone, or know the location of the nearest telephone, and be ready to call 911 if necessary.

AFTER-HOURS PRECAUTIONS

Once you have closed the store for the day and gone home, savvy store owners or managers knows they still can't let their guard down when it comes to loss prevention and personal safety. Criminals have a number of ways to con unsuspecting retailers into dangerous situations, making it critical that you keep your wits about you at all times.

Calls Back

Store owners and managers frequently receive after-hours calls requesting that they return to the store—so often that most people just accept them as a necessary hassle of doing business. Most of these calls are legitimate and pertain to such occurrences as fires, break-ins, alarm soundings, and the like, but many are not. *It is thus imperative that you not leave home before calling the appropriate official department or agency and confirm that they indeed called you.*

This will eliminate the danger of your going to the store in response to a ruse and being robbed or assaulted. If the named officials did not call you, report the matter immediately to your local police department. Pharmacists and others who operate businesses that carry merchandise required in emergency situations are especially vulnerable to call-back ruses. If you are in this category, notify your local police department of the situation before going to the store, and ask to have a police officer meet you there. Of course, don't unlock or enter the store until the officer arrives.

Break-Ins

Unless you are exceptionally fortunate, sooner or later your store is going to be broken into. When it happens, you will in all likelihood be informed of the break-in by the police. At least . . . you'll *assume* it is the police. First, you must confirm that it was indeed the police who called you. Only then should you proceed to the store—but *do not enter unless the police are there to go in with you.* Actually, it is much safer to open the door for the police and let them check out the interior of the store before you go in. If the police are not there when you arrive, withdraw to a safe location *away from the store* and notify the police that you are near the store, awaiting their arrival.

If a burglary has occurred and funds and/or merchandise are missing, or if serious damage has resulted, follow police instructions. Do not touch or disturb anything that may be used as evidence. In all cases, an itemized list of merchandise taken will be required by the police. Make extra copies for yourself, your insurance company, and other officials, as appropriate. The list should fully describe the items taken, the serial numbers (if known), the model numbers, the quantities taken, and the prices. Special notifications, of which you should be aware, must be made if items such as narcotics, weapons, explosives, or other dangerous chemicals or materials are stolen.

Occasionally, your store may be broken into during the night, possibly through the roof or a wall, in a way that avoids your burglar alarm. In this case, the burglary will not be detected until you open the store the following morning. Therefore, *one of the first things you should do when you open is to look for signs of a break-in.* Check the ceiling, air shafts, and perimeter walls. If any break-in signs are detected, immediately call the police.

Your primary purpose after a break-in is to secure the area for the subsequent police investigation. Keep customers out of the store—or at least clear of the break-in area—including the location of the illegal entry, and wherever money, merchandise, or sensitive materials may have been taken, disturbed, or strewn about. Get a rope from your emergency storage kit (described later in this chapter) and cordon off all appropriate areas. Instruct your employees not to go into or near any area that contains potential evidence until the police arrive and complete their investigation. Do not discuss the incident with anyone except the police and others who have an official reason to know details.

BANK DEPOSIT SAFEGUARDS

Most people understand they should take extra care when they're holding the day's payload of cash and checks and are on their way to the bank to make a deposit. But exactly what kinds of precautions are necessary?

Bank deposits should be made daily, and all too often, store owners and managers allow this daily procedure to become so routine and commonplace it becomes an almost subconscious activity. Receipts are gathered up, placed in clearly marked and obvious bank deposit bags, and casually carried to the bank. This is a bad and potentially dangerous habit that creates an enormous risk for the person making the deposit by making the person an easy and obvious target for a crime.

At the very least, vary the times you make the bank deposits, and conceal the deposit bag. The bags provided by servicing banks are so obvious and familiar that openly carrying one is tantamount to pleading, "Take me, take me!" Hide it inside a store shopping bag, a purse, briefcase, or under a garment.

- **If at all possible, do not make the deposit by yourself.** Make every effort to be accompanied by another employee, who should follow at a discreet distance. This way, if you are held up, your companion can summon help. The same procedure should be followed when making night deposits, especially if they are made after you close the store for the night, and even if you are driving (rather than walking) to your bank to make the deposit. Have someone follow you in another car and observe your activities until you have safely made the deposit and left the area. In addition to this individual's benefit to your personal safety, he or she could serve as a witness in case you are ever wrongfully accused of fabricating a holdup.

- **Be extra alert when dropping off deposits at bank repository boxes.** Check the surrounding area carefully. If persons in the area look suspicious or things just don't seem right, leave the area immediately. If you are followed, go to a heavily populated, well-lighted area and call the police. If you must use the night deposit box for an after-hours deposit, don't relock the box and leave before you have checked to be sure that your deposit bag disappears into the repository and is not caught or snagged in the chute.

- **Consider using the services of an armored car company.** This is especially important if your business is located in a high-crime area or in a remote area that takes you away from your store for long periods of time for bank runs. Also keep in mind that your bank business vulnerability involves more than making deposits. You're also a target by bringing large amounts of change back to the store for daily business. Those heavily laden sacks of rolled coins can be deadly giveaways, so using an armored car service can not only save you time but can reduce your overall risk of a robbery.

- **Keep records of all bank deposits.** Banks are not infallible, so it should be part of store ownership responsibility to keep a detailed record of every transaction. This may be as simple as an adding machine tape or as sophisticated as a computer program, but it should reflect the exact composition of each bank deposit that is made. Such records can be invaluable during investigations of claims made by banks that a deposit was "short"—and you would be surprised at how often this happens. Keep your records with the daily cash reports to which they pertain. Whenever a deposit is made when the bank is open, request and retain the deposit slip validated by the bank teller who handled the transaction. Validated deposit slips for night deposits should be picked up on the next bank business day and verified against your records.

NATURAL DISASTERS AND CIVIL UNREST

How many times have you watched news reports on television and wondered about the retail businesses that were looted after events that went awry? There is no need to emphasize the dangers to retail businesses of riots, war zones, and civil strife—recent history has made everyone painfully aware of them. Such outbreaks have occurred in the past and in all likelihood will occur in the future, with or without the usual accompanying violence. Add to that the risks of earthquakes or weather-related havoc in some areas, and you realize the importance of having a plan when, for whatever reason, things get crazy.

For your own personal safety and that of your employees and customers, you must stay attuned to current events in the neighborhood of your store. Confrontations and disturbances can rapidly escalate to extremely dangerous levels, and you must know how to respond. Stay tuned to local radio and television stations and to any official channels of communication; keep abreast of crowd size, direction of movement, and mood. In extreme cases, you may have to board up, evacuate, and close your store. Heed the advice of your local police department, and be aware of the following general guidelines:

- Business establishments that remain open or appear to be open during a disturbance do not suffer the same damage, looting, and fires as those establishments that close. Events, however, may require that you close for the safety of your customers and employees.
- If necessary, have people exit through a rear door.
- Keep with you as many employees as will voluntarily stay. Some may wish to remain because of a lack of safe exit or because they have no way to get home.
- Check all areas for unauthorized persons.
- Lock all outside doors, restrooms, stockrooms, and trash rooms.
- Keep all lights on in the store.
- Have flashlights (and extra batteries) ready in case of power failure.
- Collect fire extinguishers and place them near doors and windows, in case fire bombs are thrown into the store.
- Connect garden hoses to faucets that have been adapted for their use. If you have buckets or other containers that can hold water, prefill several of them to more quickly fight fires.
- Assign someone to gather first-aid supplies and place them in a pre-arranged area.
- Empty all cash registers, leaving the drawers open, and lock the money in the safe. Include money order blanks and as much high-value merchandise as will fit.
- Have employees who remain appear to be working, but keep them away from doors and windows.
- Do not stand around inside or outside the store as if on "guard duty."

Incorporate as many of these recommendations as can be applied to your business into the store's written company policies, and make them known to all employees.

BOMB THREAT GUIDELINES

At the time this book was being written, Wal-Mart stores were the targets of numerous bomb threats. Wal-Marts in Ithaca, New York; Winchester, Virginia; and three stores in Gatineau and Granby, Quebec, were just a few to be evacuated when callers notified the stores that bombs had been hidden there.

While it is true that at least 90 percent of bomb threats are malicious hoaxes, the store manager can never afford to take a chance. The person who makes the call usually wants to disrupt business by causing an evacuation, but in the tiny percentage of actual bomb placements, the caller may want to avoid loss of life by tipping off authorities.

In short, they cannot be ignored. You must know and observe the following guidelines, and go over them periodically with employees who are most likely to receive incoming calls. Setting forth this information on a card and posting it near the appropriate telephones is a good precautionary move (see Figure 1-1).

- If the threat is received by telephone, the individual taking the call should write down the exact time of the call. Record *exactly* what was said by the caller. Try to develop additional information. Can any background noises be heard? Laughter? Tinkling glasses? Loud conversations? Is the call possibly coming from inside the store? What about the voice—is it familiar? Can you determine the sex of the caller? The approximate age? Is the speech slurred, excited, or calm and rational? Do you detect any ethnic accent or unusual dialect?
- If possible, question the caller. Is the person sure he or she has the "right" store? What is the correct location of the store? What kind of bomb is it? What does it look like? Where is it? Why was it placed? What time is it set to explode? If possible, keep the individual talking and try to alert someone else so the police can be notified on another line and the call can possibly be traced.
- If the threat is received by mail or through some other written communication, keep the handling of it to a minimum to preserve evidence and fingerprints.
- Call your local police and fire departments.
- *Avoid panic.* If you or the police decide to evacuate the store, *don't* tell your customers they have to leave "because there is a bomb in the store." You might, for example, go to your light panel and turn out all the lights for a few seconds. Repeat this a few times, gradually increasing the length of time the lights are off. You can then announce with some degree of credibility that you are experiencing electrical difficulties and that it will be necessary to turn off and/or check the electrical power and evacuate the store.
- Alert the owners and managers of adjoining businesses unless you are the sole occupant of a stand-alone building.

FIGURE 1-1 Bomb threat information form.

BOMB THREAT INFO CARD
(Fold and place under or near telephone)

Date: _____ Time: _____ Location: _____

Received By: _____

EXACT WORDING OF THREAT:

_____

_____

_____

_____

_____

Length of Call: _____

QUESTIONS TO ASK:

1. Sure you have the right store?
2. Store location?
3. When is bomb to explode?
4. Where is it?
5. What does it look like?
6. What kind of bomb is it?
7. Did you place it?
8. Why?
9. What is your name?
10. Your address?
11. Where are you calling from?

EVACUATE IF NECESSARY
NOTIFY ADJOINING BUSINESSES

CALLER ID:

Sex: _____ Age: _____

VOICE:

Familiar: Yes _____ No _____

Voice sounded like: _____

_____ Normal	_____ Soft/Loud
_____ Excited	_____ Laughing
_____ Accent	_____ Slurred
_____ Rational	_____ Angry
_____ Clear	_____ Vulgar
_____ Other	

BACKGROUND SOUNDS:

_____ Street noises?
_____ Office noises?
_____ Factory noises?
_____ Animal noises?
_____ Motors/machinery?
_____ Music?
_____ Loud conversations?
_____ Clear?
_____ Static?
_____ Coming from in store?
_____ Other?

RECENT SIGNIFICANT INCIDENTS:

_____

REPORT IMMEDIATELY TO:

Police: _____

Fire Dept: _____

Bomb Squad: _____

(*Source:* ProTect)

- If a detonation time has been given, clear the premises 15 to 30 minutes before the stated time and keep the store closed until approval for reopening has been given by local authorities.
- As in all cases of emergency evacuation, assign a responsible employee to check the restrooms, basement, and stockroom areas for customers and employees who may be unaware of the danger. Lock all office funds in the safe. If time permits, collect the cash register receipts and lock them in the safe; if not, instruct employees to lock their registers and give you the keys. All employees should evacuate the store and gather at a place designated by you so you can ensure they are all accounted for.
- A search of the premises will usually be made by the police. Employees, however, because of their knowledge of their work areas, have proven to be excellent resources when searching for unusual objects. The assistance of employees in such searches must be strictly voluntary. In addition, these volunteers must be told not to touch, move, or shake anything.
- If a bomb or any unusual object is found, point it out to the police and clear the area immediately.
- If no bomb is found, do not assume it is not there. Most bombs today do not "look like bombs" at all. They can be disguised or hidden in cans, boxes, shopping bags, briefcases, and any number of common containers.
- Instruct your employees not to mention the reason for the evacuation to anyone and not to discuss the incident.
- To help the investigation, try to recall whether you or anyone else in the store had any recent experience with any customer or employee that could have caused sufficient animosity to prompt a bomb threat. If so, inform the police.

EMERGENCY KITS

Every store should maintain a well-stocked emergency kit. The contents of such kits can be invaluable for protecting the building and the assets of the store in the event of civil disturbances and other emergencies—fires, floods, power outages, break-ins, broken windows, and minor on-the-job injuries. The kit should contain the following:

- First-aid supplies. An employee trained in CPR and emergency first aid is a definite asset. Some stores require that their employees take a CPR course.
- Flashlights and fresh batteries, stored separately to prevent corrosion. In addition, flashlights should always be available in offices, in all department areas, and in all storage or backroom work areas.
- Rope or clothesline of sufficient length to cordon off the area and prevent entry into the store.

- A quantity of "No Entry" and "No Trespassing" signs that can be posted on doors and walls and tied to cordons.
- Garden hoses fitted with spray nozzles and faucet adapters, and of sufficient length to reach all portions of the store.
- An assortment of hardware items: hammer, nails, screwdrivers, pliers, duct tape, markers, knives, and scissors.

PERSONAL SAFETY CHECKLIST

Opening Procedures

❑ Check the store perimeter and surrounding area for suspicious signs.

❑ Make sure you have backup when opening the store; never open the store alone.

❑ Develop an alerting procedure so someone can check on your safety.

❑ After opening, relock the door until normal business hours begin.

Closing Procedures

❑ Lock all store funds in a safe.

❑ Empty all cash registers and leave them open.

❑ Lock and set the alarms for all rear, side, or auxiliary doors, windows, and other openings.

❑ Make a complete area-by-area check for "hide-ins."

❑ Make sure you leave the store sufficiently lighted.

❑ Test and set the burglar alarm and any other surveillance system.

❑ Before exiting, check the area for suspicious persons or activity.

❑ Never close the store alone.

❑ Make sure no one remains in the store after closing.

After-Hours Precautions

❑ Verify all calls requesting your return to the store.

❑ Notify the police and ask them to meet you at the store if you must return to handle a legitimate emergency.

❑ If you and/or members of your staff must remain in the store after normal closing hours, ensure that all exterior doors are locked and notify your local police and alarm company.

Break-Ins

❑ Check for signs of unlawful entry before opening the store.

❑ If such signs are noted, prohibit everyone from entering the store until the police arrive and make a thorough check of the premises.

Continued

❑ Check for signs of a burglary immediately after opening the store.

❑ If a burglary has occurred, make sure the area is protected and don't touch anything until the police arrive and complete their investigation.

❑ Inform all employees that they are not to discuss any break-ins with anyone except the police and others who have official reasons to know details.

❑ Make an accurate list, as soon as possible, of all merchandise taken. Make copies of the list for the police and the insurance company.

Bank Deposit Safeguards

❑ Vary the times you make deposits.

❑ Make every effort to have someone escort or shadow the individual making the deposit.

❑ Conceal or camouflage easily identifiable bank bags on the way to the bank.

❑ Check the area around bank deposit boxes for suspicious activity before approaching, especially at night.

❑ Double-check that deposits placed in night-deposit boxes do not get caught or snagged in the chute.

❑ Keep a record reflecting the composition of each deposit.

Natural Disaster or Civil Unrest Procedures

❑ Monitor current events and potentially disruptive activities occurring in the neighborhood of the store.

❑ Develop civil unrest policies and inform all employees.

❑ As applicable, follow all recommended procedures described earlier in the chapter.

Bomb Threat Guidelines

❑ Treat all bomb threats seriously.

❑ Train all employees, especially those who respond to incoming telephone calls, how to handle bomb threats.

❑ Keep bomb threat information forms near every telephone (see Figure 1-1).

❑ Make sure all supervisory and staff employees are knowledgeable regarding proper store evacuation procedures.

Emergency Kits

❑ Maintain a well-stocked emergency kit—or several, depending on store size.

❑ Be sure all employees know where the first-aid kits are located.

❑ Make sure someone on the staff is trained in emergency first-aid and CPR procedures.

CHAPTER SUMMARY

This chapter has examined key loss prevention policies and practices to protect any store owner's most important asset—the physical safety of the people who work there. Key topics included the following:

- **Opening and closing procedures.** Don't open the store alone, or create a backup procedure with a friend, spouse, or neighboring store owner to check up on you after opening. At closing time, lock cash in the safe, ensure all doors and windows are locked and that there are no hide-ins lurking. Leave lights on and, most importantly, don't close the store alone.
- **After-hours precautions.** When you get a call-back to your store, confirm that actual police or security company personnel made the call, and if in doubt, have police meet you at the store. If you are notified of a break-in, also confirm the report with the police department first. If there is any suspicion of a crime, never enter the store until and unless the police are there.
- **Bank deposit safeguards.** Don't make deposits alone; be extra alert for suspicious activity around after-hours bank repository boxes; and consider using an armored car service. Make (and keep) detailed records of every deposit. Also vary the times and the routes taken to make the bank trips.
- **Disaster and/or civil unrest procedures.** Remain open or appear to be open to minimize the possibility of attack and/or looting. Be ready to escape through rear doors. Keep as many employees as possible at the store. Check for unauthorized persons inside. Lock all outside doors and inside doors to restrooms, closets, and stockrooms to reduce the chances of hide-ins. Keep store lights on. Have flashlights, fire extinguishers, water hoses, and first-aid kits near at hand and ready to use in case of power failure or a firebomb.
- **Bomb threat guidelines.** Have a bomb threat checklist within easy reach of phones, and be sure all employees who answer the phone know how to make proper use of it in the case of a phoned-in threat. If the threat is written, handle the note and/or envelope as little as possible to preserve evidence. Notify police and fire units. Avoid panic by giving customers another "reason" for leaving the store. Clear your premises 15 to 30 minutes ahead of the declared detonation time, and be sure everyone in your store is evacuated. Leave the handling of any potential explosive device to the local bomb squad.
- **Emergency kits.** These should include first-aid supplies; flashlights and fresh batteries; garden hoses with spray nozzles; a tool kit with hammer, nails, pliers, screwdrivers, duct tape, knives, and scissors; and rope or clothesline to cordon off inside areas and/or prevent entry.

These physical safety procedures, safeguards, and guidelines represent basic knowledge retail store owners must have to establish and maintain a reasonably safe work environment for employees. It is important that you continue to increase your knowledge of physical security and refine the procedures and policies as they specifically apply to your business.

DISCUSSION QUESTIONS

1. If you get a call-back to your store, why is it important to confirm the call with the agency that made it?
2. What's the safest routine to establish when making bank deposits? Should the routine be the same during banking hours and after hours?
3. Research the services offered by armored car companies, and the cost. Are they worth the price for a smaller, single-store merchant?
4. How much of a store's banking-related information and policies do you think should be shared with employees? Explain your reasoning.
5. Research a major catastrophe of past years—an earthquake, a riot, the New Orleans flooding, and so on—and see what you can find out about its impact on the merchants in the area.
6. Why do the authors suggest you not stand around inside or outside the store as if on "guard duty" during periods of civil unrest?
7. How can you or your employees help the police catch the person who makes a bomb threat against your store?
8. What items should be included in your store emergency kit(s)? Can you think of additional items that you would include? List them and briefly explain your choice(s) to the class.

2

PHYSICAL
SECURITY

After safeguarding your personal safety and that of your employees, a retail merchant's next priority is to protect the physical security of the business and its merchandise. **Physical security** includes those actions taken to safeguard the building, premises, and physical assets of the business. Space limitations make it impossible to provide detailed data for every type of retail establishment, but the information provided in this chapter is applicable to most of them.*

Note: Depictions of security products presented in this book are for illustrative purposes only and do not constitute endorsement by the authors or the publisher. Your best sources of on-the-scene information are the professional, licensed locksmiths and security device installation firms that service your area.

The fact is that doors, windows, and other openings to the premises can be either the first set of vulnerabilities to unauthorized entry into any building or the first line of defense—if you understand their structures, installations, locking mechanisms, and alarm devices. In this chapter, we'll stress the need to establish a successful physical security program and describe the components thereof, including:

- Break-in threats
- Securing doors
- Securing windows and other openings
- Locks
- Key control

Burglary is one of the most frustrating crimes faced by the retail industry. The U.S. Small Business Administration reports that only about one-third of business burglaries are solved by identification and arrest of the perpetrators, and even when the robbers are nabbed, almost none of the cash or property is recovered.[1] It is obviously better to prevent burglaries in the first place than to become part of this discouraging statistic.

BREAK-IN THREATS

First, let's look more closely at the who, when, and why of burglaries. Generally, more data has been collected about residential burglary than retail, but the following conclusions have been drawn from law enforcement and retail industry sources:

- The typical burglar is a young man who commits a variety of predatory crimes. A small number of burglars work in groups and specialize in retail heists, disabling alarms and targeting higher-value goods; but most are not that sophisticated, and their decision to break into a business is often at least somewhat spontaneous.[2]
- More than half of these crimes occur for monetary reasons, which include the criminal's need for food, shelter, quick cash, and/or to feed his or her drug addiction.
- About one-fourth of these crimes occur for the "thrill" of it. The robber is angry or excited, wants to impress other thugs, accepts a dare, or is high on drugs and sometimes unaware of the real consequences of his or her actions.[3]

The burglar is, above all, an opportunist—always looking, literally, for that "window (or door) of opportunity." Burglars make a practice of testing

WHAT MAKES A STORE A BURGLARY TARGET?

Surprisingly few incidences of burglary or robbery are planned, but the perpetrators do show some care in selecting their retail targets. They look for locations that

Are quiet (few employees and/or customers)

Seem to be easily accessible (a busy street corner makes the getaway easier)

Have high cash flow

Are lacking in visible security measures

Are familiar to the robbers and close to their homes

Have been successfully robbed by others in the past

Are deserted on nights, weekends, holidays

Have an ATM machine

Sell thieves' "preferred" products (cigarettes, music and video products, liquor, electronic goods, designer clothing)

Are new in business (and presumably, inexperienced)

Sources: Compiled from *"Burglary of Retail Establishments,"* by Ronald V. Clarke, a publication of the U.S. Department of Justice Office of Community Oriented Policing Services (COPS) program, Washington, D.C.; and the Georgia Retail Association, Lithonia, Georgia.

all doors and windows to see whether any have been left unlocked or unsecured and might allow easy entry. If unsuccessful, burglars move on to the next stage—using force and/or the most basic tools to gain entry to buildings, as discussed in the sidebar "What Makes a Store a Burglary Target?"

- **Kicking.** A few hard kicks in the vicinity of the lockset will open many doors—the door frame breaks away, or the screws holding the strike plate to the frame pop loose. Some burglars don't even bother with trying to kick open the lock; instead, they concentrate on kicking out the panels of the door itself, particularly if the door is thin, hollow, and/or poorly constructed.
- **Shimming.** Burglars use **shimming** almost exclusively to defeat locks that consist of only a latch bolt—that is, the type of locking mechanism that is beveled and will retract under pressure. All a burglar has to do is slide a *shim*, a thin piece of metal or plastic (even a credit card) between the lock and the frame, and the door can be easily opened.

- **Jimmying.** A screwdriver, prybar, or even a tire iron is all that a burglar needs to force open or "**jimmy**" a lock. Such tools are usually used on doors that don't fit well in their frames and are equipped with locks that have short latches or dead bolts. The tool is forced between the door and the frame, and leverage is applied to separate the locking bolt from the frame.
- **Sawing.** The next step up from jimmying, this method employs the use of a hacksaw blade to defeat locks that, although they may be mounted on ill-fitting doors, use longer dead bolts that prevent jimmying. The hacksaw is used to cut through the dead bolt or cut into it far enough so that it will yield to kicking.
- **Pounding, prying, and pulling.** This is really the use of brute force. The lock, and often the door itself and the hinges, are attacked with a variety of tools—sledgehammers, pipe wrenches, heavy pieces of metal, cinder blocks, or large stones. You name it and if it's handy and can serve the purpose, a burglar intent on entry will use it.
- **Ram raiding.** This is the term for driving a motor vehicle (usually stolen) through windows, doors, or even building walls in perhaps the ultimate "pounding" technique. It became somewhat common in the mid-1990s, but calls so much attention to itself that it is generally used as a last resort or by thugs bent on malicious destruction of property.
- **Drilling.** This is less the forte of the "common" burglar and more the realm of the professional—especially when the lock to be drilled out, with the aid of sophisticated tools, is affixed to a safe or vault. **Drilling** out a lock on a perimeter door is a snap for most professional burglars. Unfortunately, the field is expanding and includes many semiprofessionals who use the wide variety of cordless electric drills now on the market to drill out locks and gain entry.
- **Picking.** In this method, the burglar, usually a professional, uses a set of thin metal rods with hooks on the ends of them for **picking** a lock. The rod is inserted into the keyway as a key substitute, and is then manipulated and turned so as to align the pins in the lock cylinder. Once the pins are aligned, the locking mechanism can be turned, thereby moving and retracting the latch or dead bolt and opening the door.

Now that we know how burglars get in, let's take a look at specific building vulnerabilities and see what can be done to correct them.

DOORS

Poorly constructed, inappropriate, ill-fitting, and improperly installed exterior doors are not just a hassle for store owners and employees, they are a virtual invitation to burglary, making it relatively simple for thieves to enter the store. A close examination of the existing doors, followed by some simple precautions and modifications, can put the odds back in your favor.

First, take a close look at the door frames. Even the heaviest of steel doors are worthless if they are attached to weak, split, or rotted wooden frames. Repair or replace them immediately if you note such conditions, preferably using metal frames.

Next, examine the hinges that secure the door to the frame. Can you see them with the door closed? If you can, and they are on the outside (as they are in many old buildings), you may have a problem. There is no need for burglars to pick your lock or cut holes into the door panels to gain entry, if all they have to do is remove the screws holding the door to the frame and lift off the entire door in one easy operation. Have the door rehung so that the hinges are not visible, or at the very least, replace the old slotted screws with one-way, nonre-tractable screws as soon as possible. While you are at it, replace the hinges with new hinges that have no removable pins. You'll thwart an easy tapping out of the hinge pin and removal of the door in that manner. To be really secure, have the entire assembly welded to the door, and to the frame.

Doors are vulnerable not only through their frame, hinges, and lock as-semblies but also through structural deficiencies and inappropriate use. Unfortunately, many hollow-core and lightweight wood-paneled doors designed for interior use are improperly installed as exterior, point-of-entry doorways. Primary doors should always be of metal or solid-core wood con-struction at least 2 inches thick, without panels and with a good, tight, flush fit to the door frame. If there are glass panels within 40 inches of a lock, it is possible that the glass could be broken and the lock jimmied. Either replace the glass with a solid panel or with one of the types of security glass de-scribed in this chapter, in the section on windows.

Don't concentrate all your attention on your front door; your rear and side doors are more likely to be challenged by burglars because such doors are usually located where burglars can work unobserved. If you are in a mul-tistory building, don't forget about the upper-level fire exit doors. Can they be reached from the ground on pull-down ladders?

Simple supplemental devices especially suitable for rear and side doors can be utilized to provide additional break-in protection. One of the most common devices is a bolting mechanism that is either surface mounted or internally mounted on a door, with the bolt extending into the frame. Metal bars or sturdy wooden bars can also be installed on the door's interior, with the bars extending beyond the frames. In addition, steel pins and bolts may be installed on the sides and tops of doors that have corresponding holes in the door frames; this prevents criminals from prying the door off or lifting it out of its frame. Figure 2-1 is an example of a high-security door with a multilocking mechanism.

Although these safeguards pertain mostly to preventing entry when the store is closed, some doors must also be protected during business hours.

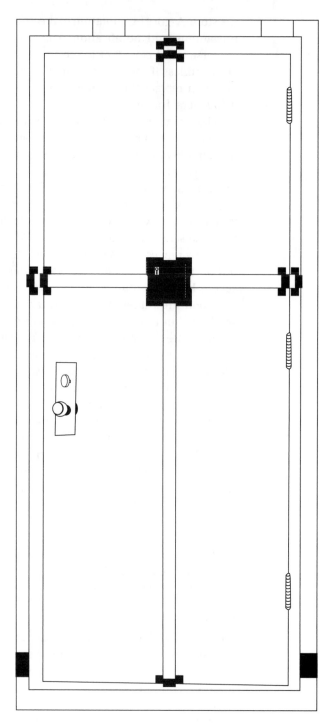

Figure 2-1 Door with four-point locking system.

In most situations of this type, owners rely on appropriate alarm systems, but, as will be discussed later, other actions may be necessary. For example, if rear doors must be open for ventilation, it may be necessary to install an additional door constructed of metal bars or heavy screening and secured from the inside by a key or other locking mechanism. The use of peepholes, door chains, and door guards, which allow a door to be opened only 2 inches, may also be appropriate. (Are you sure that the man ringing the bell at your rear receiving door is really a delivery person? Take a look and check him out before you fully open your door and let him into your store.)

Every store should have only one primary point of entry, and because it's usually the most visible, it should be the front door. The keyways of all other exterior doors should be plugged or rendered inoperative and otherwise set up so that they can be opened only from the inside. This procedure will not only make it more difficult for burglars to gain entry, but, just as important, it will prevent after-hours reentry by dishonest employees who have access to or have made their own unauthorized duplicate keys.

WINDOWS

Windows present different problems than doors. Unless you want your store to look like a fortress, you will have large expanses of windows, both for display purposes and to create a bright, pleasant shopping atmosphere. Even when a window has an alarm, it doesn't take long for a thief to throw a trash can through the glass, climb into the store, grab merchandise, and be gone before the police arrive. Other than resorting to the use of metal roll-down protective covers and scissor-type grilles that are almost mandatory in high-crime areas (and during periods of civil unrest), there isn't much you can do to minimize these types of illegal entries, other than keeping the interior of the store well lighted at all times.

However, if the building is yours to alter and the budget permits, consider using security glass or safety glass. Available types include the following:

- **Laminated glass.** A vinyl or plastic layer is sandwiched between two layers of glass, adding extra strength. Laminated glass deters burglars because they must hit it repeatedly in order to get it to break and, of course, the noise involved makes them less likely to attempt it.
- **Tempered glass.** Regular glass is superheated and then chilled, in a technique that is also used to make sturdy, restaurant-quality glassware. A tempered glass window is four to five times stronger than regular glass.
- **Wired glass.** Wire mesh is embedded in glass or sandwiched between glass plates, again adding strength and discouraging burglars, who can clearly see the wire they'd have to cut through. While not appropriate for display windows, it works well for others.[4]

Technology has made some types of security glass suitable for display purposes; it has the additional benefits of noise suppression, which is especially nice for stores in busy areas, and protection from sunlight exposure to displayed merchandise. Security glass can be expensive, though, and it cannot simply be installed in place of regular glass. Instead, the panels are set in a frame and the whole frame is installed in the window opening.

Unless they must be opened periodically, all windows in the store—especially those that cannot be seen from the office or main sales floor—can be permanently closed. Bolt them to the frame with **lag bolts** (with the bolt heads recessed) to prevent their being removed as a unit. Then protect them with half-inch round steel bars secured in the masonry at least 3 inches. Follow that by covering the entire assembly with heavy wire mesh. You are striving here to create a defensive situation that will not only prevent burglars from crawling in but will keep shoplifters and dishonest employees from throwing merchandise out, to be retrieved later. This goes especially for windows located in relatively private areas such as lavatories, back hallways, and stockrooms.

If you have windows that must occasionally be opened, keep them secured with the type of sliding bolt lock that uses a combination padlock as the locking mechanism. Keep the combination confidential, known only to store management.

OTHER OPENINGS

Frequently overlooked in the perimeter protection planning process is the identification and safeguarding of miscellaneous openings in your store—ventilation shafts, air ducts, skylights, and trap doors—that allow for surreptitious entry. The protection methodology for such openings usually consists of both locks and alarms, with emphasis on the latter. (They are mentioned here, rather than in the section devoted to alarm devices, in order to provide you with a better understanding of your total perimeter vulnerabilities.)

■ **Ventilation shafts and air ducts.** Many burglars use shafts and ducts to enter stores, especially when access to the shafts is from the roof. It's a simple matter to remove a shaft cover or duct hood, secure a rope (or have a partner hold it), and drop or crawl down into the store, so these openings must be protected. If at all possible, do this from the point at which the duct or shaft originates. Use heavy-gauge wire mesh or steel bars welded or bolted to the frame or roof with nonretractable bolts. In the same manner, secure the endpoint of any shaft or duct that could allow entry into the building. As an added measure, these openings should be incorporated into your store burglar alarm system. Your alarm installer will use a wire grid method called "trapping" to protect such areas.

- **Skylights.** No matter how handy the daylight they provide, skylights also provide criminals an even easier way to enter your store. Protect them in similar fashion as shafts and ductwork.
- **Trap doors.** In most buildings, a number of small doors provide access to the roof. These must be locked and alarmed.
- **Common walls.** The **common walls** referred to here are those separating your business from those of your adjoining business neighbors. It may seem odd to be discussing common walls in a section captioned "Other Openings." However, all too often, common walls abutting neighboring businesses are overlooked or not closely examined. If your business is located in a strip mall or a building that has had a lot of tenant movement and renovation, pay particular attention to your common walls and the crawl space above your ceilings. Frequently, you will find that what you assumed to be a common firewall extending to the roof line is a partial wall or "**short wall**" that extends only a short distance above the ceiling. This type of construction is another open invitation to the savvy burglar. The burglar can easily remove or slide open a ceiling panel on one side of the wall, crawl up and over, and come down on the other side—right into your store. This is one vulnerability that may be used by dishonest employees of adjacent businesses, especially if entry may be gained from rear storage areas and provides access to your stockrooms. Many merchants have lost thousands of dollars' worth of merchandise to such "ghost thefts" and never knew why. Don't let it happen to you!

Most short walls are noted by local fire marshals, but many are not. If you have a short-wall problem, get together with your business neighbors, building owner, and/or management company and correct it. If a wall cannot be properly extended to the roofline, try to have some heavy metal bars or heavy-gauge wire screening installed. At the very least, bring it to the attention of your alarm installer so that the area can be "trapped" and properly safeguarded with contacts and a grid of alarmed wires.

LOCKS AND KEYS

Once the right type of door or window is selected and properly installed, the next line of defense is the locking mechanism that secures it from opening. Where should locks be installed and what type(s) should be used?

The first part of that question is easy to answer. All **perimeter doors** that allow access into the store should be protected by locks. Recommending a specific type of lock, however, becomes a bit more difficult. Gone are the days when the choices were either a simple padlock or some sort of key-operated handle or knob mechanism. Locks now range from relatively simple combination or push-button devices to complex electromagnetic systems operated by a variety of coded card readers and remote signals. There are even locks that operate on a voice-recognition signal; still others, used to protect extremely sensitive areas, are activated by precoded thumbprints or palm prints. Selecting the types that are best suited for a particular retail location depends in part on the lines of merchandise, and the store owner's budget, and the choices should be made with the assistance of a competent, licensed locksmith.

To be able to discuss your needs with a locksmith, you should know something about the more common locking devices available and the primary uses for which they are intended. Such knowledge will also help you to better understand and evaluate the locksmith's recommendations. Keep in mind that a locksmith is not a mind reader. Certain types of stores may have specific lock requirements because of their layouts or types of merchandise, and these should be discussed with the locksmith. Locksmiths are, after all, a bit like doctors—they can't provide the cure unless you can describe all the symptoms. Remember to comply with all of your local building code requirements, especially those affecting the functions of locks used on fire doors and emergency exit doors.

Types of Locks

It is possible to take a look at the world of locks without getting too technical. However, in order to make sense of this section, you'll need the following definitions:

- **Latch bolt.** The angled or beveled end of the lock mechanism that projects from the front of the lock. When the door is swung shut, the extended latch bolt slides into a hole in a metal plate (the strike) affixed to the door frame. The locking mechanism can be configured to work by simply turning the door knob, or by using a key or a thumb latch. This is the most common type of locking mechanism. It is used most frequently on locks for interior doors leading to closets, bedrooms, and bathrooms. It is also among the least secure locking devices—it can easily be defeated by sliding a shim, such as a thin piece of metal or a credit card, between the door and the frame and against the beveled latch. When used on an entry door, a latch bolt must be backed up with another type of lock that will provide much better protection. (See Figure 2-2 for a sketch of a latch bolt.)
- **Dead bolt.** The part of the locking mechanism that protrudes from the lock body. When extended (or "thrown," in locksmith jargon), it fits into a hole cut into a metal plate (called a **strike** or **strike plate**) attached to the door frame. The primary feature of the dead bolt is that, unlike the latch bolt, when a dead bolt is in the closed (locked) position, the bolt will not retract with end pressure. Dead bolt use is strongly recommended for all store perimeter doors, stockrooms, offices, and other areas where a higher

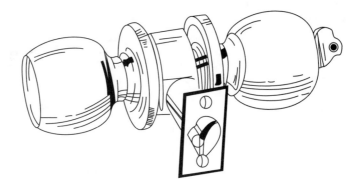

Figure 2-2 Typical latch bolt lock.

degree of protection is necessary. Locks using the dead bolt principle are made for a wide variety of purposes and come in many styles and configurations. Some examples are shown in Figures 2-3, 2-4, and 2-5.

- **Cylinder.** The subassembly of the lock, which contains the locking mechanism. (See Figure 2-6.)
- **Core.** The portion of the lock assembly containing only the **keying plug** (the area into which the key fits) and the **tumbler** mechanism. The cores of many locks are removable for easy replacement (an extremely desirable feature). (See Figure 2-7 for a sketch of a core assembly.)
- **Tumbler (or pin tumbler).** The part of the locking mechanism that is contained within the core. It consists of a number of short, spring-activated rods, commonly referred to as pins or tumblers. The more pins or tumblers a lock has, the better it is—because the harder it is to pick. When the pins are properly aligned by the turn of a matching key, the mechanism

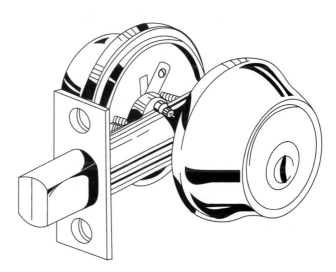

Figure 2-3 Cylindrical dead bolt lock.

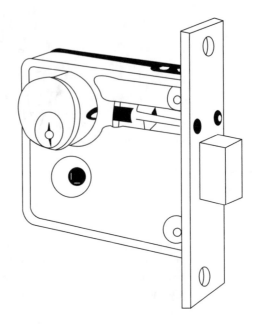

Figure 2-4 Mortise dead bolt lock.

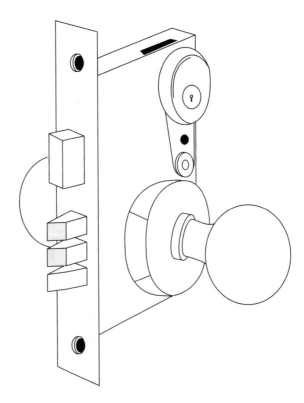

Figure 2-5 Dual latch bolt and dead bolt lock.

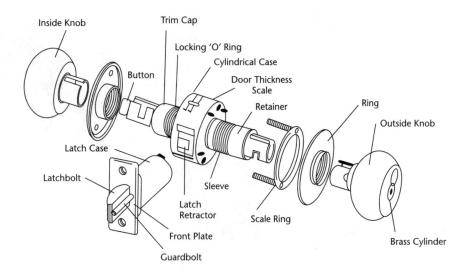

Inside Knob
Trim Cap
Locking 'O' Ring
Cylindrical Case
Button
Door Thickness Scale
Retainer
Ring
Outside Knob
Latch Case
Sleeve
Latchbolt
Latch Retractor
Scale Ring
Brass Cylinder
Front Plate
Guardbolt

Figure 2-6 Cylinder assembly.

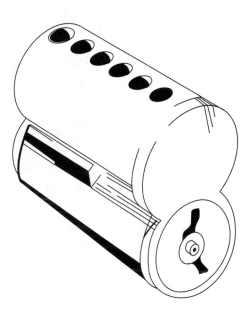

Figure 2-7 Lock core.

becomes operational, and the latching device, such as a dead bolt, can then be extended to lock the door or retracted to unlock it. (Figure 2-8 is a closer look at a pin tumbler assembly.)

- **Strike (or strike plate).** A metal plate fastened to a door frame; a bolt or latch projects into the strike.
- **Strike box.** The housing, including the space in back of the strike, used to enclose and protect the bolt and the bolt opening. Strike assemblies should be mounted with long (at least 2½- or 3-inch) screws. (See Figure 2-9 for a diagram of a strike assembly.)

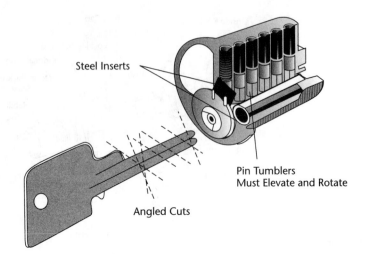

Steel Inserts

Pin Tumblers
Must Elevate and Rotate

Angled Cuts

Figure 2-8 Pin tumbler
assembly.

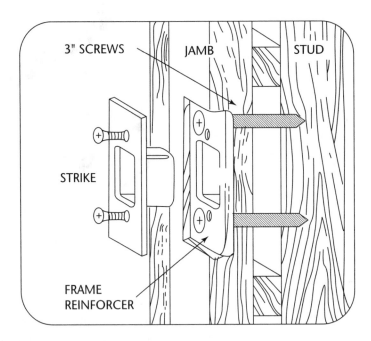

3" SCREWS   JAMB   STUD

STRIKE

FRAME
REINFORCER

Figure 2-9 Strike assembly.

- **Cylindrical lockset.** The most common type of door lock. It consists of a locking mechanism enclosed within a cylindrical chamber and mounted to a door through a large, bored hole. It usually has a knob or handle on each side of the door. (See Figure 2-10 for an example of this type of lockset.)
- **Mortise lockset.** A type of locking mechanism, usually rectangular, mounted within the outside edge of a door frame (the **stile**). Most glass

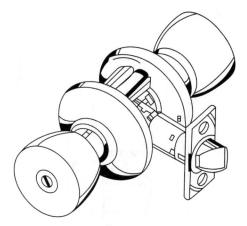

Figure 2-10 Cylindrical lockset.

and narrow metal-framed store doors utilize mortise locksets. The higher-quality locking systems include two locking mechanisms: a doorknob with a latch bolt assembly (for open-hours convenience) and a separate key-operated dead bolt lock. (Figure 2-11 is an example of this type of lockset.)

- **Slide bolt.** This is the name for the thin, metal dead bolt lock often seen in home use or, for example, in public restroom stalls. It is installed on the inside surface of the door, and the bolt is pushed into place manually to lock and unlock. For business use, it is strictly an ancillary precaution to a larger dead bolt or more sophisticated lock system. A slide bolt that is installed at the top or bottom inside edge of a door is called a **flush bolt**.

Figure 2-11 Mortise lockset.

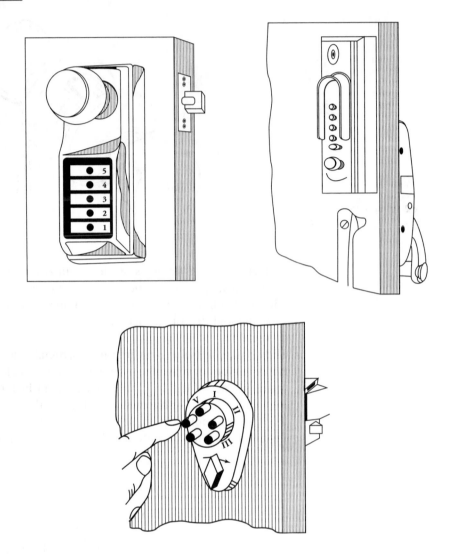

Figure 2-12 Push-button-operated locks.

■ **Auxiliary and specialty locksets.** A generic description of secondary locks, usually of the dead bolt variety, used to reinforce the primary lock. The term is also used to describe locks that, although they may operate on the latch bolt or dead bolt principle, use different activating mechanisms and are often designed for specific and unique purposes. Included in this category are locks that operate by push buttons, magnetic card readers, and a wide variety of remote control electromagnetic and electromechanical release devices, and several different types of dead bolts that mount on exterior doors. Locking devices for fire doors and emergency exit doors are also in this group, but because of their specialized nature, they will be discussed later in this chapter. (For examples of the wide variety of auxiliary and specialty locks available, see Figures 2-12 through 2-15.)

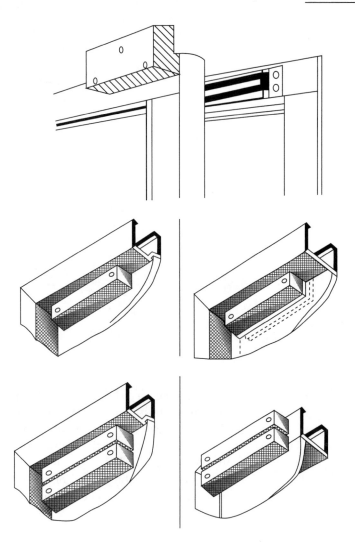

Figure 2-13 Electromagnetic locks.

Padlocks

As a locking device, padlocks are in a class by themselves. Their varieties and purposes are almost endless. They range from the very simple, easily picked types to the most complex of combination, special-keyed, and shielded varieties. Figures 2-16 and 2-17 are examples of the variety of padlocks available.

Padlocks have one major drawback: they must be mounted on something—called a **hasp**. The strongest padlock in the world is worthless if it's mounted on a hasp that can easily be pulled apart or pried away from its fasteners. A strong mounting hasp, properly secured, is an absolute must when using padlocks. Get one that comes with a hinged locking bar that, when in place, conceals the mounting screws, as shown in Figure 2-18.

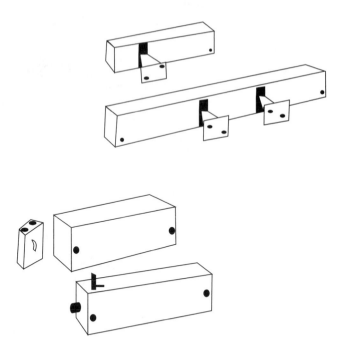

Figure 2-14 Electro-mechanical locks.

The padlock itself should be sturdy, too—preferably operating with a pin tumbler mechanism. The case and the **shackle** (the curved bar that attaches the lock to a hasp) should be made of hardened steel. For extra protection, consider using a sturdy, high-security combination padlock. If a door or area protected by a padlock is to remain open for any length of time, relock the padlock on the mounting hasp. This will prevent anyone with ulterior motives from switching the lock and reentering later.

CHOOSING LOCKS

Unless yours is a very modern building with advanced security controls, its doors—particularly at primary points of entry—are most likely going to be the mortise type and key-operated (shown in Figures 2-11 and 2-4, respectively). Depending on the business environment, a store owner may choose to use a locking device activated by a magnetic card reader or a push-button lock that requires the user to punch in a combination of numbers.

Regardless of the type of operating mechanism, insist that the lock have a dead bolt with at least a 2-inch extension (the sliding part of the lock that goes into the frame or stile). If the primary lock does not have a dead bolt, install a second, auxiliary lock that does. Think about your own residence—isn't there an additional lock installed on the door of your home or

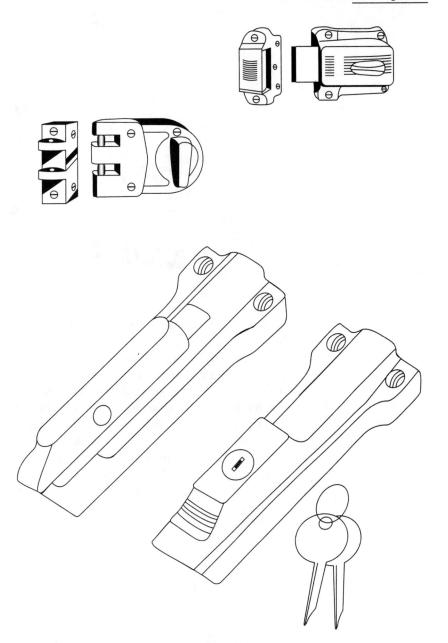

Figure 2-15 Surface-mounted bolt locks.

Figure 2-16 General-purpose padlocks.

apartment? (If not, there should be!) You should provide similar protection for your business.

If possible, insist the locks are of the pin tumbler type, with at least five pins, and that the core cylinder is easily removable and interchangeable. In the event you feel the key to the lock has been compromised—that is, someone has had improper access to it or may have had it copied—you can immediately change the locking mechanism and the key by *switching the core with a spare set kept on hand in your safe.*

As previously mentioned, all perimeter doors other than the one point-of-entry door should be made inoperable from the outside. In addition to being alarmed and secured with a variety of bolts, bars, and chains, these

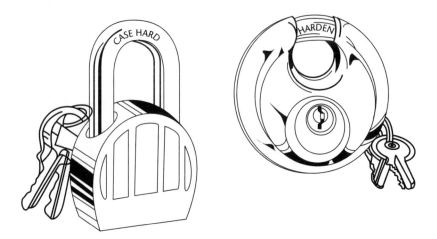

Figure 2-17 High-security padlocks.

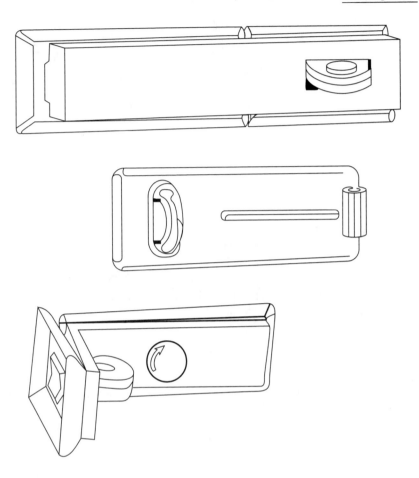

Figure 2-18 Hasps with hinged locking bars.

doors must also remain locked. Strong, key-operated dead bolts are preferable, but padlocks are used in many such situations.

Fire Doors and Emergency Exits

Special attention must be given to locking devices installed on doors designated as fire or emergency exits. This subject will be addressed in detail in a later discussion of alarms, but some general warnings are in order here.

- Scrupulously obey all fire regulations and building codes relating to fire doors and emergency exit doors. Equally important, see to it that your employees obey them.
- Do not chain, bolt, padlock, or otherwise affix any type of device to one of these doors that can hinder it from quickly opening from the inside in the event of an emergency.

Rim Devices

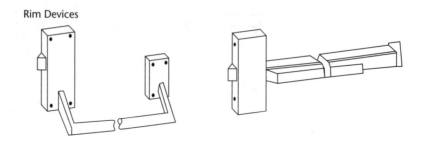

Mortise Devices

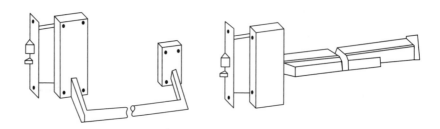

Concealed Vertical Rod Devices

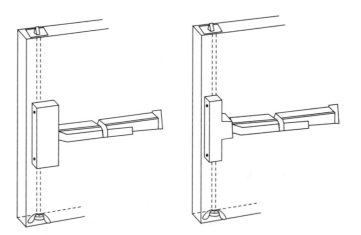

Figure 2-19 Emergency exit devices.

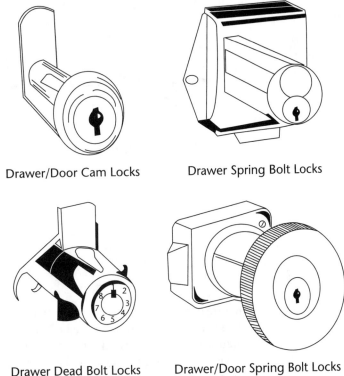

Drawer/Door Cam Locks   Drawer Spring Bolt Locks

Drawer Dead Bolt Locks   Drawer/Door Spring Bolt Locks

Figure 2-20 Drawer and cabinet locks.

- Do not block the door by stacking merchandise, trash, or other materials in front of it. Be sure the hallways leading to the doors are clear.

By law, all emergency doors must be equipped on the interior side with some type of broad panic bar or paddle that, when pressed or pushed against, immediately opens the door. When necessary, the exterior of the door can be equipped with a keyway to operate the locking mechanism. (See Figure 2-19 for examples of emergency exit devices.)

Other Locked Areas

In addition to perimeter doors, other areas that should be secured by locks include offices, stockrooms, and, where possible, restrooms. Cash drawers and cabinets containing security-sensitive or high-value merchandise should also be locked. Figure 2-20 shows examples of drawer and cabinet locks. **Showcase locks**, to secure the sliding glass doors of display cases, are also available, as shown in Figure 2-21.

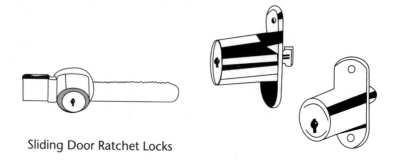

Sliding Door Ratchet Locks

Figure 2-21 Sliding door
locks.

Sliding Door Plunger Locks

TIME LOCKS

Before concluding this discussion of locks, we must mention one more type. The **time lock** referred to here is different from the type commonly associated with bank vaults and safes. Instead, this type of time lock is a secondary device that must be unlocked to gain entry into the store, and only the store owner has the key.

In a retail store environment, the purpose of a time lock is to prevent internal theft by employees—more specifically, by the management staff. If the nature or size of the business requires that employees work various shifts or the store owner must rely on someone else to open or close the store, a potential theft problem exists. Unless the store installs a card-reader locking system that automatically monitors and records each time a door is opened, or contracts with a central station alarm system company to notify the owner of every instance when the burglar alarm is turned off during periods when the store is closed, the store is vulnerable to unauthorized reentry and theft of merchandise by dishonest managers and assistant managers. Retailers that shrug off the need for an alarm system altogether are truly courting disaster. They *really* need a time lock!

Attached to the point-of-entry door, the time lock provides the store owner with a written record of all after-hours entries. Mere installation of such a lock acts as a powerful deterrent to internal theft.

KEY CONTROL

As practical and as sturdy as they may be, the major drawback to any key-operated lock is that it is only as good as the control exercised over the key.

Because of this vulnerability, certain keys should be exclusively retained and controlled by store management. They are the keys to:

- Locks on front and rear entry doors
- Locks on high-value stockrooms
- The manager's office
- Any company-owned delivery vehicles.

Every store should have a key plan. All major lock companies manufacture locks that can be keyed for different degrees or levels of access:

- The **grand master key** is the owner's or manager's key. It can open all lock groups that have been keyed to work with it.
- The **master key** is the department manager's key. It can open all lock groups within one specific department or area that have been keyed to work with it.
- The **individual key** is used by general employees. It will open only one lock, or perhaps a series of cabinets or showcase locks, located within the employee's immediate work area.

Many lock manufacturers make key-operated locks that allow the key to be removed only when the lock is in the secure or locked position. These locks, referred to as **captive locks**, are excellent choices for cash drawers. Most cash registers and point-of-sale terminals utilize such locks. Having the key in the lock is a graphic reminder to the responsible employee that the drawer can be opened.

A number of lock companies make high-security keyed locks with unique keying mechanisms that can only be operated by keys that have been precisely and specially cut. Duplicate or replacement keys for such locks cannot be made on standard key-cutting machines. They must be ordered from the factory, where the lock and its owner are registered and strict accountability is maintained.

If key loss or replacement is a problem, the company should seriously consider one of the many combination, push-button, cypher, or card-reader locks that are currently available. These locks eliminate the aggravation and worry of lost or stolen keys. Equally significant, they allow quick and frequent changes of their operating codes, a desirable and strongly recommended practice.

Even if you don't need to resort to such a high level of security, there are a number of other key control practices that you should follow:

- Limit the number of keys issued.
- Number the keys. To instill in your employees a sense of responsibility for key care, number each key issued. Simple-to-use metal stamping kits are available at most hardware stores. Require each employee to sign a receipt for each key received.

- Maintain a log of keys issued. At the very least, the log should reflect the date of issue, the name of the individual receiving the key, the location of the door or cabinet for which the key was issued, and the key number. The log should also have a space to note whether the key was returned when the employee is transferred or terminated, or resigns.
- Stamp "Do Not Duplicate" on all keys issued.
- Do not tag keys with the store name or with any address.
- Conduct periodic (at least quarterly) inventories of all keys issued.
- Re-key locks periodically under normal conditions. Re-key immediately at the time of departure of supervisory personnel and when other employees leave under less than favorable circumstances.
- Keep unissued and spare keys in a safe to which only you have the combination, or in a separate, locked cabinet. A number of good key cabinets are available. Some, in addition to being very secure and fireproof, contain automated access, monitoring, and dispensing devices. An example of such a system is shown in Figure 2-22. Other key control systems are depicted in Figure 2-23.

The sales and cashier staff members must be instructed about proper key control procedures. Cash register keys must be pulled out and retained by the person responsible for each register or terminal, when duties take him or her away from the immediate vicinity. The key should not be put into another register drawer, on a shelf or a hook or—the typical method—in a box beneath or behind the counter. These actions only have to be observed once to leave the register wide open to thieves, who can strike the next time they find the register area unattended. Even more frequently, they profess interest in an item, and while the salesperson scampers to the back stockroom to check for a particular size or color, the con artist is busy cleaning out the register.

The keys to showcase locks also require special handling. They should be kept in the register drawer of the salesperson on duty. At closing time, they should be turned in with the day's receipts and locked in the safe. These actions will prevent the keys from being found and used when the department is not staffed or during a break-in.

Managers should carry only those keys necessary for the daily operation of the store. Infrequently used, excess, or duplicate keys should be tagged and left in a safe or in a secure key cabinet. It's also good advice for store owners and managers never to carry all their keys on one ring. Divide them into groups—for example, an exterior group (perimeter doors, time lock, bank deposit box, and so on) and an interior group (stockrooms, register reading keys, day alarms, and so on). This practice will deny dishonest employees any opportunity to open rear doors and throw merchandise outside to an accomplice or for pickup after they leave the store. They won't be able

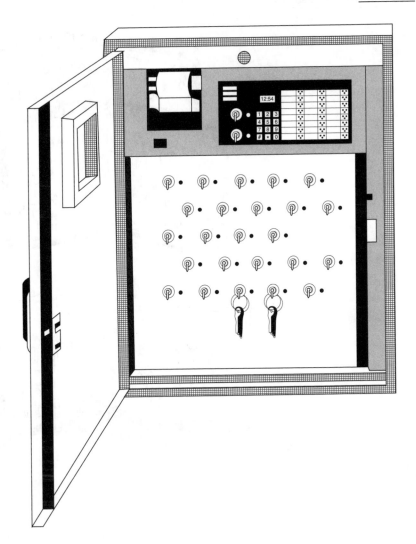

Figure 2-22 Security key
monitor.

to copy exit door keys while supposedly only needing and using the key to
a stockroom or other internal area.

If you are going to be away from the store for an extended period of
time—on vacation, on a buying trip, or for medical reasons—leave your set
of keys in the safe unless they are going to be used in your absence by a
trustworthy manager.

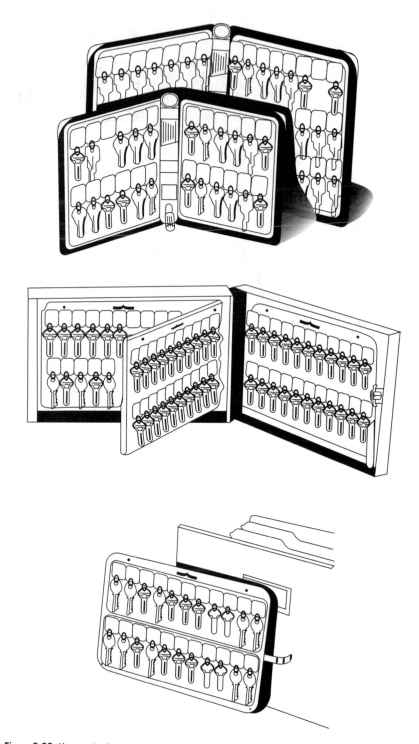

Figure 2-23 Key control systems.

PHYSICAL SECURITY CHECKLIST (PART ONE)

Doors, Windows, and Other Openings

❏ Protect all doors, windows, and other openings to store premises with locks, alarms, or both.

❏ Make sure all door frames are sturdy and in good condition.

❏ Make sure all doors are hung properly. They should fit in the frames snugly with the hinges well secured, and the hinge pins should be protected from easy removal.

❏ Install supplemental locking devices on all rear and side doors.

❏ Designate only one door as the primary point of entry.

❏ Make sure all windows that don't need to be opened occasionally are permanently closed and bolted to their frames. In addition, protect them by installing steel bars and wire screening.

❏ Consider the use of security glass in at least some windows.

❏ Use locks to secure any windows that must be opened occasionally.

❏ Lock and install alarms on all ventilation shafts, air ducts, skylights, and other potential openings to the building.

❏ Examine the common walls adjoining other businesses, to ensure that no crawl spaces or short walls allow surreptitious entry into your store.

Locks and Keys

❏ Examine the locks on all doors, to ensure they are of the proper type and are properly installed.

❏ Reinforce latch bolt locks by installing a more secure dead bolt lock.

❏ Use key-operated locks of the pin tumbler and interchangeable core cylinder types.

❏ Install dead bolt locks that have extensions (bolts) of at least 2 inches.

❏ Securely mount the strike plate into which the dead bolt fits with long (at least 2½- to 3-inch) screws.

❏ Make sure the locks to all perimeter doors (other than the one point-of-entry door) are inoperable from the outside.

❏ Use only padlocks made of hardened steel. If they are not of the combination type, make sure they operate with a pin tumbler mechanism.

❏ Ensure that mounting hasps for padlocks are sturdy, well secured, and conceal the mounting screws when in place.

❏ Pay special attention to locks installed on fire exits to be sure they can be opened immediately in case of emergency.

Continued

❏ Properly lock offices, stockrooms, cash drawers, and cabinets containing security-sensitive or high-value merchandise.

❏ Equip your primary point-of-entry door with a time lock to detect unauthorized entries after the store is closed.

❏ Establish a key plan by keying the locks for different degrees or levels of access.

❏ Maintain a log of keys. Require employees to sign receipts for all keys issued.

❏ Conduct periodic key inventories.

❏ Properly secure spare keys.

❏ Train all employees in proper key control procedures.

❏ Segregate store management keys and give managers only those keys necessary for the daily operation of the store.

❏ Consider replacing key-operated locks with combination, push-button, or magnetic card reader locking devices.

CHAPTER SUMMARY

In this chapter, we have examined the key loss prevention policies and practices to safeguard the building, premises, and physical assets of a business, including:

- **Break-in threats.** Eliminate the vulnerable access points that burglars seek for easier entrance to your store. Think like a thief as you critically examine your premises for ways to defeat the kicking, shimming, jimmying, sawing, pounding, prying, pulling, drilling, or picking that would allow access to the building.

- **Doors.** Correct your door vulnerabilities by making sure outer doors, door frames, and hinges are properly constructed (solid), fitted and installed, and lockable. Pay particular attention to side, rear, and fire exit doors.

- **Windows.** With front windows, you face a "security versus service" dilemma, so if you can't use roll-down protective covers or scissor-style grilles, put alarms on the windows and keep the area around them well lighted at all times. Look into the possibility of replacing display windows with security glass; other windows not used for display may be permanently closed with lag bolts, bars, and/or steel mesh. If they need to be opened periodically for ventilation, windows can be secured with sliding bolt locks that use combination padlocks.

- **Other openings.** Use steel mesh, nonretractable bolts, locks, and, especially, alarms to secure ventilation shafts, air ducts, skylights, and trap doors. Pay particular attention to common walls between your business and others that may have "short walls" in the crawl spaces above your ceilings. Whether or not you coordinate with the other businesses, secure these areas with bars, heavy steel mesh, and/or alarms.

■ **Locks.** All perimeter doors that allow access into the store should be protected by locks. Many interior areas should also be lock-protected, and all installations must comply with local building and fire/emergency evacuation codes. Lock types include latch bolts, dead bolts, cylindrical dead bolts, mortise dead bolts, padlocks, and specialty locks that include time locks, push-button locks, magnetic card readers, and a wide variety of remote control electromagnetic and electromechanical release devices. Whatever locks you choose, make perimeter door locks inoperable from the outside except for your point-of-entry door.

■ **Key control.** Key-operated locks are only as good as the control exercised over the keys that open them, so keys must be carefully tracked. Use grand master keys, master keys, and individual keys to limit employee access only to their areas of responsibility. Stamp "do not duplicate" on all keys issued, limit the number of keys issued, maintain a key log, don't identify keys with store name/location tags, and keep a tight inventory of unissued keys. Periodically re-key your locks, or if yours is a business in which key control is a problem, consider push-button, cipher, and/or card reader locks instead of traditional keyed locks.

DISCUSSION QUESTIONS

1. Why is it important to "think like a burglar" when inspecting a building for possible ways of unauthorized entry?
2. What common door vulnerability is most often exploited by burglars?
3. Describe a security problem unique to businesses with mall or strip shopping center locations.
4. What are three important considerations when deciding on the types of locks to use for a retail business?
5. Who should have ultimate control over key issuance and storage, and why?
6. How does a store owner reconcile the dual priorities of making employees feel valued and trusted, while also "keeping an eye on them" for signs of criminal activity?
7. Should a retail store have a budget specifically for security items like locks and keys? Find out what some of the costs are for typical locksmith services in your area.
8. Knowing what you now know about locks, keys, and common entry points for thieves, look at your own house or apartment with these

points in mind. List and describe at least three ways in which your home security might be (or has been) improved.

ENDNOTES

1. *Curtailing Crime Inside and Out,* U.S. Small Business Administration, Washington, D.C.
2. Ronald V. Clarke, *Burglary of Retail Establishments,* Office of Community Oriented Policing Services (COPS), U.S. Department of Justice, Washington, D.C., March 13, 2002.
3. National Institute of Justice, Washington, D.C., 1996.
4. TBO-TECH Self-Defense Products, Inc., Fayetteville, North Carolina.

ALARM SYSTEMS AND OTHER PHYSICAL SECURITY MEASURES

This chapter addresses specific loss prevention polices and procedures associated with the variety of **alarm and detection systems** needed by every business.

Alarm systems come in a wide variety of configurations ranging from the simple to the highly sophisticated and technically advanced. A business owner's decisions about an alarm system will depend on his or her store location, merchandise type and value, and the financial resources that can be devoted to this important part of the overall security plan.

In this chapter, you will learn how alarms and detection systems are installed, how they operate, and how they support and supplement the basic physical safety and security steps presented in the first two chapters of this book.

Specific subject areas to be covered in this chapter include the following:

- Burglar alarms
- Day alarms
- Holdup alarms
- Specialized alarms
- Fire, smoke, and equipment-related alarms
- Closed-circuit television
- Security lighting
- Disposal of sensitive documents

BASIC ALARM TYPES

There are three basic types of alarms and signaling devices:

1. **Local alarms** sound a siren, bell, or loud horn on the premises or in the immediate vicinity of the area or merchandise being protected.
2. **Central station alarms** are silent at the premises, but they transmit a signal through leased telephone lines to the police or to a private security company's monitoring office.
3. **Direct-dial alarms** work through electronic devices and existing telephone lines to send prerecorded messages to protection agencies, police and fire departments, and others.

Let's examine the adaptability of these various systems and devices to the retail store environment and at the same time take a closer look at their basic structures and general use.

BURGLAR ALARMS

Most burglar alarm systems are two-stage configurations consisting of a primary or perimeter alarm system and a secondary or space alarm system.

Perimeter Alarm Systems

The **perimeter alarm** is the most common and most familiar alarm system. It protects against unauthorized entry through the exterior shell of the

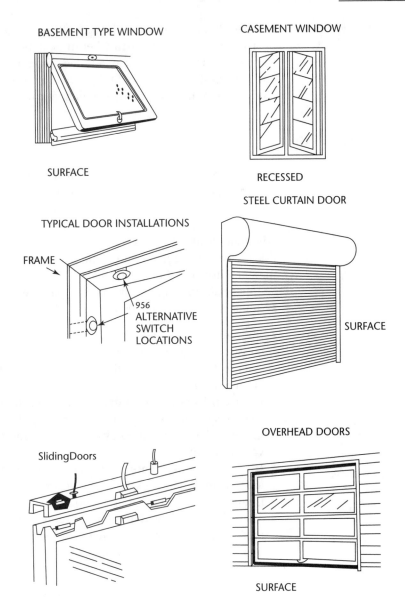

BASEMENT TYPE WINDOW

SURFACE

CASEMENT WINDOW

RECESSED

STEEL CURTAIN DOOR

TYPICAL DOOR INSTALLATIONS

FRAME

956
ALTERNATIVE
SWITCH
LOCATIONS

SURFACE

SlidingDoors

OVERHEAD DOORS

SURFACE

Figure 3-1 Magnetic contact applications.

building, by using magnetic contact devices and magnetic foil tape affixed to all doors and windows that can be opened. Figure 3-1 shows the wide variety of applications suitable for such devices.

Sound, vibration, and motion detection alarm devices can also be used to monitor penetrations through roofs, walls, and large expanses of glass. Ventilation shafts, skylights, and trap doors leading to the roof can be alarmed in the same manner. These areas can also be protected using an alarmed **wire trap**, a grid made of wire that triggers an alarm when it is touched. A variation of the wire trap is the **switch mat**, a thin, wired, matlike device that signals an alarm when it is stepped on. The advantage of the switch mat is that it may be concealed—under carpets in entryways, foyers, and hallways; on stairways; and so on—so it is well worth considering as an alternative to the easily damaged magnetic foil tape alarm sensors.

Space Alarm Systems

Also known as an **intrusion detection system**, a space alarm provides a secondary zone of defense against criminals who manage to penetrate the basic perimeter system. It can detect the movements of burglars who have gained entry by jimmying locks or crawling through air shafts and false ceilings of adjoining establishments. It will also detect "hide-ins" and "bust-outs"—thieves who hide and remain in the store after closing, gather up money and merchandise, and then break out to be picked up by accomplices.

Space alarms range from relatively simple mechanisms to sophisticated systems. Without getting too technical, these alarms are described as follows:

- **Photoelectric systems.** Commonly used to open doors, these systems consist of a light beam aimed at a receiving cell, and the activation of an electrical current. When the light beam is crossed and interrupted, an alarm is transmitted.
- **Passive infrared motion detection systems.** These are similar to photoelectric systems except that the infrared light beam is invisible. Changes in infrared energy, caused by an intruder's interruption of the beam, activate the alarm.
- **Ultrasonic motion detection systems.** Inaudible ultrasonic sound waves are transmitted into a specific zoned area. Any movement within the zone is reflected back to the sending unit, causing the alarm to be activated.
- **Microwave motion detection systems.** Similar to ultrasonic systems, these systems can be zoned to cover specific areas. They use the Doppler effect—detecting a shift or interruption in frequency—to signal a change that triggers an alarm.

Ultrasonic and microwave motion detection systems both have advantages and disadvantages. On the plus side, they are excellent devices for detecting intruders inside the store and can be "zoned" to protect an entire store, or any portion thereof. On the minus side, they are frequently plagued by false alarms caused by any number of common conditions: noise and vibrations from within or outside the store, power failures, birds, the janitorial staff at work after hours, air currents from heating and air-conditioning ducts, and so on. On the whole, however, most false alarms are caused by user error, poor or inappropriate installation, and/or inferior equipment.

Regardless of their occasional problems, secondary intrusion detection systems contribute significantly to a total physical security protection package. Their installation is not a do-it-yourself job; there are too many variables to take into account in terms of planning and device selection, as well as the installation itself. The services of a professional alarm company are almost certainly required.

Choosing a Burglar Alarm System

Should a retail store's burglar alarm system use the local alarm or the central station alarm type of notification system? The answer depends on your goals and your operational environment. Do you just want to scare burglars away—or do you want to catch them?

Local alarms, which ring loudly enough to be heard throughout a neighborhood, work well provided there are neighbors around at night to hear them. The other critical variable is what the neighbors *choose to do* about the alarm they hear. If they are not fed up with false alarms and/or the failure of store management to reset the system so they can get back to sleep, will they call the police? Or will they assume, as too often happens, that someone else has already called?

Although local alarms are the least expensive of the notification systems, they should be used only in areas where response times can be rapid, such as in shopping centers with security patrols or in metropolitan areas with high degrees of municipal police coverage.

Silent, central station alarm systems are preferable. They are more expensive to install and maintain, but they usually pay for themselves in the long run. Activated without the knowledge of the intruder, they allow police in quick-response areas to catch burglars in the act of breaking in or while they are inside the store, which makes arrest and prosecution easier. Silent alarms have a strong deterrent effect. Word gets around quickly when a store has an effective alarm system, thus reducing the store's chances of being targeted in the future.

One caveat: Never let a burglar alarm system lull you into a false sense of security. Many professional thieves today are technology-literate and some of them have learned to defeat—or at least compromise—most alarm systems. Frequent alarm examinations and tests are recommended, and a backup system may be advisable. Even so, today's merchants must be alert to individuals posing as alarm system salespersons or alarm maintenance personnel, especially if they ask to inspect your system. They could very well be burglars, or be gathering information for other criminals. Check them out before sharing even the most basic information about your alarm system.

DAY ALARMS

Compared to the alarm systems previously mentioned, **day alarms**, or open-hours alarms, serve a completely different purpose. Day alarms are installed to detect break-*outs*, not break-*ins*. They are installed on exit doors to provide additional protection against shoplifting when the store is open; they alert store management or security if someone tries to steal merchandise and exit through one of the alarmed doors. There are two basic types of day alarms: the local alarm and the remote alarm.

Local Alarms

As its name implies, the local alarm is part of the door locking mechanism, and often can be purchased with the security door. These devices come in a wide variety of configurations and designs, but their common denominator is that, when someone activates a local alarm by pushing the panic bar or paddle that locks the door, a loud bell or buzzer sounds.

One of the more desirable features found on some of these exit-device alarms is a delay feature that sounds the alarm as soon as the panic bar/paddle is pushed, then does not allow the door to be opened for 10 or 15 seconds. This delay only slightly slows immediate exit in case of emergencies, but usually allows enough time for store security to respond to an unauthorized door-opening. Examples of some local exit door alarms are shown in Figure 3-2.

Remote Alarms

Remote alarms are usually installed on fire exits and other exterior doors. These exits are located far enough away from the main sales floor that a local alarm built into the door might not be heard. Remote alarm devices usually consist of a set of magnetic contacts similar to those used in a primary burglar alarm system. The result, essentially, is a separate secondary alarm system; instead of being activated after closing, it is active while the store is open.

A control box contains the alarm device, and the system can be turned on or off at this point by using a toggle switch or key. In addition to being the heart of this system, the control box can, unfortunately, also be its weak link. If the store owner or manager does not exercise vigilance over the control box to ensure that the system is turned off only for controlled functions, such as deliveries and trash removal, the store will soon become victim to shoplifters and/or dishonest employees working independently or in concert with others.

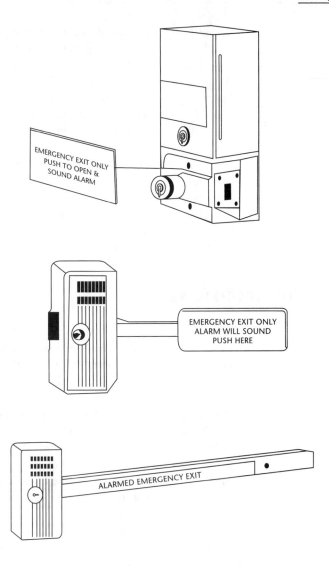

Figure 3-2 Local exit door alarms.

HOLDUP ALARMS

Almost all holdup alarms are central station or direct-dial alarms; they send silent signals or prerecorded messages to police or protection agencies, notifying them of a holdup in progress. The mechanism that activates these alarms is usually installed in a manager's office or cashier's cage, or at point-of-sale (cash register) locations. It may be a switch, push-button, foot-pad, or some other type of pressure-sensitive device.

Store owners can utilize another type of holdup alert, which is commonly known as a **buddy system**. If you are fortunate enough to have a "good neighbor" store owner nearby (preferably right next door), it is relatively simple to set up a two-way buzzer system. Each merchant buddy keeps (in his store or on his person) a panic transmitter that can be activated in case of a holdup or emergency. Pushing the "buddy button" activates the alarm, and a low-key buzz sounds in the neighboring store, alerting the other store owner to discreetly see what's going on—and call the police if necessary. This also prompts the "buddy" to note the physical descriptions and license plate numbers of any suspects and/or cars seen leaving the area.

Of course, it is important that the "buddies" establish the rules and parameters for use of their alarms including, when triggered, specific procedures for what to do next.

ALARMS FOR SPECIFIC NEEDS

The average store owner does not usually require technically advanced and expensive alarm systems to protect merchandise. On the sales floor, almost any item can be protected with a combination of showcase locks, security cables, and a wide variety of electronic antishoplifting disks, tags, and devices. However, there are specific objects or types of merchandise in some stores that deserve individual alarm protection.

The safe, for example, should be guarded by an alarm. Space alarms that detect sound or motion provide adequate protection in most instances, but a business owner wishing to protect safes containing large amounts of money or exceptionally valuable or desirable merchandise (such as jewelry, gemstones, precious metals, guns, prescription drugs, and so on) should consider other options.

In addition to safes that can only be opened at specific times, there are now electronic **proximity alarms** and **vibration detection alarms** that send signals to the police or to a central station if the slightest motion or vibration to the object is sensed. Another type of alarm is activated by the presence of human body heat. These newer types of alarms are often used to protect valuable pieces of art and high-value technical and scientific equipment.

FIRE, SMOKE, AND EQUIPMENT ALARMS

Local laws and regulations, such as building codes and fire codes, will dictate what types of fire alarm systems a business may install and perhaps mandate some basic standards, although a retailer may generally install enhanced systems at his or her discretion. The city or county, as well as any

SAFES

As the repositories for the lifeblood of the business—the money (and sometimes high-value merchandise)—safes deserve some additional attention. Not only should they be alarmed and fire-resistant, but some thought should go into their placement, installation, usage, and access.

- **Bolt the safe to the floor.** Unless you have a vault-type safe built into the structure of the building itself, this anchoring is important, especially if the safe is located near a display window. Countless safes have been removed by burglars who, using a tow truck, back up through a window, hook up the safe, and jerk it out. They then open it at their leisure in a remote location and discard it after removing the contents.

- **Open the safe only when necessary.** When it is not in use, lock it. Don't just close the door; spin the dial on the combination lock (which, of course, every safe should have). Protect the combination carefully. Don't write it down on a desk pad or a calendar, or in an address book, even if you attempt to disguise it as a telephone number. Memorize it, and give it out very judiciously. *The more people who have access to the safe, the more difficult it will be to establish responsibility in case of loss.*

- **Consider how the safe is used and what's in it.** If you keep company books, documentation, and computer disks (be sure to keep off-premises backup copies) in addition to cash, money orders, and similar negotiables, you should think about using a **dual-compartment safe**. These safes have a high-security compartment protected by a combination lock for the money and valuables, and a separate, larger compartment, protected by another lock, for the documentation and other bulkier items. Compartmentalized safes are also a way to further restrict access to the contents.

company that insures the business, often also require periodic inspections or tests of the alarm system.

Tremendous advances have been made in fire and smoke detection systems. Some are now so sensitive that they can literally "sense" fire, "hear" flames, and detect the slightest wisp or whiff of smoke. Generally, these detection devices work on the photoelectricity or ionization principle—some have interchangeable sensing units and can work either way. The alarms are calibrated to sense a buildup of heat, the presence of smoke, and the fumes and by-products of a fire, whether fast-burning or smoldering. Rate-of-rise and fixed-temperature thermostats are also available. These secondary devices are commonly used in boiler rooms, trash rooms, and areas where overheating machinery or spontaneous combustion are hazards.

As with burglar alarms, fire and smoke alarms can be installed to sound an alert on the premises and to immediately send a signal to a central station monitoring unit. To provide for the safety of customers and employees, all large stores should also install fire alarm pull stations, especially in rear storage areas.

In addition to fire and smoke alarms, many stores require alarm systems to monitor various functions and equipment. It doesn't take long, for example, for a grocer to suffer a major loss when the refrigeration system fails. Other equipment frequently monitored includes boilers, generators, elevators, sump pumps, and fuel supplies. The potential for water leaks or the possible presence of toxic gases is reason enough to install this kind of alarm protection.

CLOSED-CIRCUIT TELEVISION SYSTEMS

Closed-circuit television (CCTV) is essentially a monitoring system, but it can, and frequently does, serve also as a "visual alarm" of sorts. In addition to providing valuable videotaped evidence of shoplifters and armed robbers, CCTV is useful for monitoring rear entrances, shipping and receiving docks, and sales floors. It can also aid in detecting dishonesty among employees, particularly those who handle cash.

CCTV comes in a variety of forms, too, from armored outside units to mini-cameras small enough to be hidden just about anywhere. They may be hooked up to live feeds, digital recorders, transmitters, and receivers in any of several combinations.

When properly installed and used, CCTV systems can serve as crime deterrent devices. Early in 2005, however, the CCTV trend received a bit of a setback when a British study was released that disputed the crime-fighting merits of CCTV systems. The British government has been active since the 1990s in funding the placement of more than 4 million video cameras in a massive crime reduction effort. But the study results from 14 local camera projects in shopping centers, parking lots, residential neighborhoods, and hospitals found that only in parking lots did the presence of cameras make a difference in actual crime reduction.[1]

Until recently, CCTV also had some technological drawbacks, including poor image quality, limited storage capacity, and relatively high cost. However, technical advancements have made it possible today for even small-store owners with small security budgets to have CCTV systems that just a few years ago were only available to large companies with big budgets.

LIGHTING

Burglars do not like to be in the spotlight—literally or figuratively—so good lighting of a retail store, both inside and out, is a strong deterrent to break-ins. Sufficient interior lights should be left on at night so police patrols and other passersby can see what is going on inside the store. Don't lose this advantage by putting so much merchandise or so many "Sale" signs on the windows that it's impossible to see into the store. Make sure you have a battery-operated backup lighting system that immediately activates when interruptions to your normal power system occur. A secondary gasoline-powered or diesel-fueled generator is even better.

The exterior of the store should be well lighted; this includes front and rear, plus side entrances. A good security lighting system does not mean blasting the neighborhood with harsh, intrusive illumination that seems to simulate daylight all night long! The International Dark-Sky Association, an advocacy group for intelligent lighting design, says in the United States alone, we waste more than $1 billion annually on poor lighting. The group's recommendations for smart, security-minded outdoor lighting include the following:

- A well-shielded low-pressure sodium (LPS) fixture, which provides well-controlled light, energy efficiency, and excellent visibility with no glare.
- A high-pressure sodium (HPS) or metal halide (MH) fixture.
- Well-controlled and installed floodlights or spotlights.
- Infrared sensor spotlights that come on when someone walks into the field of view of the infrared (IR) detector, installed to put the light only where it is needed—not shooting up into the sky, or onto neighbors' property.[2]

Motion-activated lights may be a better option in some locations than dusk-to-dawn lighting, which is also controlled by a light sensor but stays on all night, every night, costing more because it uses more energy.

Set the lights high enough that the bulbs cannot be easily removed or broken, and choose lighting fixtures with wire mesh grilles and shatterproof glass. The idea is to make them (more or less) impervious to breakage from stones and pellet guns.

FIRE, ELECTRICAL, AND WATER HAZARDS

Nothing is quite so dispiriting as the first morning-after look at a store that has been reduced to rubble by an overnight fire. It is especially gut-wrenching if the fire could have been prevented.

Don't wait to make fire prevention a priority until the local fire department or insurance inspector comes around with an annual checklist. Check things out yourself, now. Make a formal tour on at least a quarterly basis, and observe the following daily fire prevention precautions:

- **If smoking in retail stores is not already illegal in your area, prohibit smoking in your store.** If an outright prohibition is impossible, do not allow smoking in the backrooms, restrooms, or near the trash storage areas.

If allowed in coffee-break areas or lunchrooms, insist that employees use glass or ceramic ashtrays, not paper or Styrofoam cups. At closing time, check the contents of all ashtrays and trash cans, and look beneath all tables and chairs for any smoldering butts. It is much easier to ban smoking on the premises altogether than to put up with the fire risk—let alone the odor and health issues associated with inhaling secondhand smoke.

- **Make sure merchandise is not stacked against or too near incandescent lightbulbs.** At least 24 inches of space is recommended. The same holds true of placing merchandise (particularly janitorial supplies, paints, and other chemicals) near hot-water heaters, motors, and electrical devices or outlets.

- **Check for signs of frayed wiring on POS terminals, lighting fixtures, and electrically operated displays.** Instruct your employees to be alert for such hazards. Check the main electric panels in the store. If they are hot or seem unusually warm, notify a professional electrician immediately.

- **Exercise extreme caution if you must use portable heaters to keep your store personnel warm in exposed locations.** Be sure to give the heaters adequate clearance from trash cans, paper bags, and other flammables. At closing time, be positive the heater is not just turned off, but *unplugged from the outlet.* If an extension cord must be used, be sure it (and the entire circuit into which it is plugged during work hours) can carry the increased electrical load.

- **Keep clear all rear areas and hallways leading to fire exits.** By law, fire exit doors must be able to be opened from the inside by means of a panic bar; they must not be locked during business hours. In fact, in many jurisdictions not even secondary locks to protect against break-ins during nonoperating hours are allowed to be locked during business hours. (These restrictions are another reason why fire exit doors should be tied into both the store's primary alarm and day alarm systems.) Check with the local fire chief for the rules in a particular area.

- **Locate fire extinguishers in every store, in conformance with local fire regulations.** Extinguishers should be available for ready access near front and rear exits, stockrooms, basement areas, and heating and electrical equipment. Although most of them require recharging only on an annual basis, check them periodically throughout the year. Know how to operate them. Be sure that all employees know the location of the fire extinguisher nearest to their duty stations and, equally important, that they know how to use it. This should be part of employee orientation and ongoing training. Test them.

- **Install fire and smoke detectors.** Test them periodically, on a schedule.

- **Develop evacuation procedures and train all employees.** This will ensure that, in case of a real evacuation, it can be accomplished in a calm and orderly manner. Customers exit first, through rear fire exit doors if necessary. Two preappointed searchers, one male and one female, should check the restrooms, stockrooms, and other areas, to alert customers and employees who may not be aware of the danger. Lock the office funds in your **fireproof safe**. Collect and lock up the cash register receipts, if time permits. If not, tell employees to lock their registers and to give you the keys. As employees evacuate the store, designate a meeting place where they are to remain until you can check later and be sure to account for all of them.

■ **Immediately after a fire, rope off the affected area or erect barriers to prevent unauthorized persons from entering.** This is necessary not only to prevent injury but also to protect against theft and vandalism. Be especially watchful that clean-up crews do not "accidentally" remove undamaged or salvageable merchandise along with the rubble. Regretfully, it is also recommended that you keep your eye on the firefighters. Most are completely trustworthy, but there have been incidents where merchandise was pocketed, tucked into boots, and removed from the store while firefighting equipment and hoses were being gathered up after a blaze.

Water Damage

Another area of serious potential loss to a retail business is water damage. Obviously, water damage is unavoidable in the event of fire, and many store owners are distressed to find that the water used to put out a fire often causes as much destruction as the fire itself.

But what is truly amazing is how much damage one overflowing sink can do in one night to merchandise, fixtures, ceilings, and carpeting. Therefore, it's very important at closing time to make sure that all faucets are turned off. Check the restrooms to see that commodes are not overflowing or that a disgruntled employee or vandal has not plugged up the basins and left the water running. If there are any old, rust-encrusted water or sewage pipes in your store, see if they leak, as this is a sign that they may be about to burst. In cold climates, be sure exposed pipes are adequately protected from freezing.

SENSITIVE-DOCUMENT DISPOSAL

The concluding topic in this chapter is perhaps the most overlooked area of physical security: that is, the safe disposal of confidential documentation. We all know the horror stories about identity theft and related problems when criminals sift through trash to find "useful" information—social security numbers, credit card slips, and so on. Retailers are prime targets for the latter. The same criminals also look for business information, including possible cash flow details or order forms that indicate what's in stock.

Beyond the fact that a store owner might be legally liable for mishandling a customer's private information, you have to ask yourself: Is there anything in the daily or weekly trash that could tip off potential burglars or other criminals about what's in the store after hours, where it's kept, or what types or brands of alarm systems you're using? The same goes for potentially dishonest employees: Does the company Dumpster include information that could make an "inside job" easier and thus, more likely?

Fortunately, securing the trash is usually much easier and cheaper than securing employees or premises. Low-cost shredders are available at any office supply store, and using them faithfully significantly reduces the chance of inside or outside theft resulting from a security leak. A more expensive (but even more secure) option is to hire a **sensitive-document disposal** or **document destruction** company. These professionals help businesses set up a document security plan and then securely dispose of documents.

PHYSICAL SECURITY CHECKLIST (PART TWO)

Alarms

❑ Install burglar alarms to protect the building's exterior shell.

❑ Install space alarm systems to detect intruders who have been able to penetrate the basic perimeter system.

❑ Install a silent, central station type of alarm system.

❑ Install a day alarm, or open-hours alarm, system to detect break-outs and unauthorized exits by employees.

❑ Install holdup alarms.

❑ Make sure the safe is protected by a proximity or vibration detection alarm.

❑ Install fire and smoke alarms.

Lighting

❑ Light the exterior of the store at night, especially the areas surrounding all doors and windows.

❑ Choose lights that are efficient and effective, including infrared sensor and motion-detector models.

❑ Make sure the interior of the store is also sufficiently lighted at night, so that police patrols and passersby can see what is going on inside the store.

❑ Install an emergency lighting system.

Fire, Electrical, and Water Hazards

❑ Educate all employees on all fire, electrical, and water hazards.

❑ As applicable, follow all safety recommendations in this chapter.

CHAPTER SUMMARY

In this chapter we have examined the loss prevention polices and procedures associated with the variety of alarm and detection systems needed by every business, including:

- **Burglar alarms.** The chapter introduced and explained the three primary types—local, central station, and direct dial—and explained the need for a two-stage system of protection, for the perimeter of the building and the interior space.

  ◇ **Day alarms** are not for burglars and break-ins, but to thwart shoplifting when the store is open and discourage employee theft. The choices here are local alarms that sound a loud bell or horn at the point of security breach, and remote alarms that sound elsewhere, within earshot of management or security personnel but not heard by the thief.

  ◇ **Holdup alarms** are the manual alarms that notify police and security agencies of a holdup or robbery in progress when an employee pushes a panic button or steps on a security mat. The importance of the "buddy system" with neighboring store owners was also stressed.

  ◇ Safes, jewelry, precious metals, firearms, and other high-value merchandise should have **dedicated alarms** that detect proximity, vibration, and movement in their vicinity. They are generally direct-dial or central station systems.

  ◇ **Fire and smoke alarms** must meet local fire safety laws and building codes. These systems range from very basic to sophisticated alarms that literally "sense" fire, "hear" flames, and "smell" smoke. These systems can sound local or remote alerts and are generally linked to central stations.

  ◇ **Closed-circuit TV** is generally a monitoring system that can be used as a visual alarm and a deterrent to employee theft. Today's CCTV systems are far more capable and less expensive than just a few years ago, but their overall effectiveness has been questioned.

  ◇ Good **lighting** deters burglary, but "good" does not necessarily mean the brightest, most annoying lights in the neighborhood. This chapter mentioned the need for lighting design and introduced a few of the better choices for external security lighting.

- **Sensitive-document disposal.** Criminals can "case" a business by searching its trash for clues about assets and security systems. Eliminate this security threat before, during, and after document disposal, by limiting employee access, shredding documents before they go into the trash, or hiring a document destruction company to provide those services.

DISCUSSION QUESTIONS

1. What is the difference between local, central station, and direct-dial alarms?
2. Describe the difference between a burglar alarm and a day alarm.
3. How does a store set up a "buddy system" holdup alarm? What kind of merchant would you choose as a "buddy?"
4. Why should you have separate alarm systems for your safe and other high-value targets inside your store?
5. Find out more about CCTV and formulate an opinion about whether it is useful in retail, or whether merchants' money could be spent more effectively on other crime-reduction tactics. Explain your thoughts in a paper of 700 words or less.
6. What is the most overlooked area of physical security, and how do you address it?
7. Research the area of security lighting, and describe what you think would be "intelligent" external lighting for a retail business.
8. What types of policies do you think a retail store should have for storing and/or shredding confidential documents relating to credit card trans-actions? Employment files?

ENDNOTES

1. Jim Lawless, "British Study Says CCTV Cameras Don't Deter Crime," Associated Press, London, February 25, 2005.
2. International Dark-Sky Association, Inc., Tucson, Arizona.

4

SHOPLIFTING

Shoplifting accounts for about 14 percent of the more than 7 million larceny-theft offenses in the United States each year. In calculating federal crime figures, shoplifting is lumped in with pickpocketing and purse snatching, thefts from vehicles, buildings, and vending machines, and thefts of bicycles. Generally, these are not high-dollar crimes—the average larceny theft is around $700, and the typical shoplifting incident nets merchandise less than $200 in value—but all together, they total losses of at least $5 billion per year and probably more.[1]

Its very nature makes the crime of shoplifting especially tough for merchants to pursue. For the most part, it is a minor, nonviolent offense that neither causes public outrage nor fear. While it probably annoys the general public because people understand on some level that it raises prices, there often isn't much sympathy for the huge retail conglomerate that prosecutes an individual shoplifter.[2]

This chapter addresses the policies and procedures any retailer must establish and follow to reduce shoplifting losses, which, given the wide-open, self-service environment in most retail establishments, can be a real challenge. Specific subject areas to be covered in this chapter include the following:

- Shoplifter personality types
- Shoplifting methods and suspicious behavior
- Preventive measures
- Confronting, detaining, and arresting shoplifters
- Care and control of shoplifting evidence
- Making court appearances

It's an unpleasant fact of life that anyone who comes into your store could be a potential shoplifter, or **booster** as they are commonly known by law enforcement personnel. Shoplifters come in all sizes, shapes, ages, and socioeconomic groups. Professionals do it for a living; substance abusers do it to support their habits; kleptomaniacs do it to satisfy a compulsive urge; and disgruntled customers or employees do it for revenge or to "get even" for some real or imagined slight. Sadly, the elderly, the unemployed, and the homemaker may resort to shoplifting out of desperation, to supplement lean budgets or momentarily ease depression. Juveniles do it to stretch their allowances, as initiation into clubs, on a friend's dare, or just for "kicks."

HOW SHOPLIFTERS WORK

The methods and techniques used by shoplifters to separate a store from its merchandise are limited only by imagination and resourcefulness—which, unfortunately, they have in great abundance. The specific acts may vary, depending on the circumstances, but shoplifting is usually carried out in one of three ways: (1) sleight-of-hand, (2) devices, and (3) distraction.

Sleight-of-Hand

Also known as **palming**, this is the most common method used to shoplift, especially by nonprofessionals. Despite connotations of the term from the world of magicians and performers, sleight-of-hand is not nearly so exotic. Items are simply and quickly taken by hand and concealed in sleeves, pockets, or purses, or dropped into shopping bags or other packages.

Devices

For the most part, devices are used almost exclusively by professional shoplifters. A schoolgirl who hides lipstick in a hollowed-out schoolbook is technically using a "device," but the ones we are focusing on here are much more elaborate and devious. For example, a wide variety of **booster coats** feature a number of pockets and hooks sewn into the lining, enabling them to hold and conceal great quantities of merchandise. A companion garment is the **booster bloomer**, a large undergarment tied at the bottom around each leg and worn under loose fitting clothing. An amazing number of silk dresses, for example, can be dropped into and concealed in such a device. There are also **booster boxes**, devices disguised to look like ordinary garment boxes, boxes ready for mailing, or gift boxes. Their unique feature is that the bottom or one end is false or spring-operated. The shoplifter places the box on or near the targeted item, pushes it against the box, and, like magic, it disappears.

Some shoplifters are rather colorfully known as **crotch carriers** because they are skilled at carrying merchandise between their upper legs. A proficient thief can carry out astonishingly heavy and bulky items in this manner; a few even use slings under their clothing to support heavy loads.

Strollers and baby carriages—especially the older, larger types—are favored devices of many female professional shoplifters. The carriages are modified so the mattress or pad on which the baby rests is raised, leaving a large space underneath for the concealment of shoplifted goods. Often, the "baby" in the carriage is a doll, not a real infant.

Distraction

Working in pairs or in larger groups, these shoplifters employ a wide variety of ruses to distract managers and sales personnel from their duties. Some are very simple, like the one where a pair comes into a department area and, while one engages the salesperson in showing merchandise or retrieving an item from a stockroom, the other shoplifts.

A common group technique is to create disturbances by engaging in loud arguments and mock fights among themselves, or having a group member fake a fainting spell or a seizure. Then, while everyone clusters around to see what is going on, the rest of the team cleans out the store.

Another type of shoplifter—the so-called **clean shoplifter**—is particularly costly to deal with if security personnel are not wary. Clean shoplifters are not really shoplifters at all; they just want you to *think* they are. They act suspiciously or even take and conceal merchandise openly—then leave the items elsewhere in the store or pass them off to an accomplice before being confronted by some unwary manager or salesperson. Then, after they are found to be "clean," they initiate civil lawsuits for false arrest, malicious prosecution, or defamation of character. Large monetary settlements can result from such tactics.

PREVENTIVE MEASURES

The key word here is *preventive*. Except in those rare cases when you really want to catch someone in the act and make an arrest, your goal should be preventing shoplifting, not watching it occur. To successfully accomplish this goal, however, you must have a dedicated and knowledgeable management staff and a motivated, trained, and alert sales force.

One of the best ways to accomplish this is to develop a reputation for being a **tight store**—that is, a store in which it is difficult to shoplift. There are various shoplifting deterrent devices, psychological procedures and barriers, and store layout strategies that can help you accomplish this. Some guidelines are provided in the following sections, and all of your employees should be trained to make use of them throughout the workday.

Customer Relations

- **Promptly acknowledge the presence of all persons who enter the store or department.** Even if you are engaged with another customer, make some comment, such as "Good morning, ma'am," or "I'll be with you in a moment, sir." This is a win-win technique: Your true customers will appreciate your interest; those intent on shoplifting will know you're watching them.
- **Give quick service.** This is another win-win tactic that greatly reduces the opportunity and the temptation to steal (especially important where juveniles are concerned).
- **Assist customers who carry merchandise around the store in their hands.** Offer to help them by holding the items or by getting a cart. If you see an item being dropped into a pocket or a purse, mention it by name. For example, "May I hold these items and that lipstick for you?"
- **Instruct and periodically remind all cashiers to check the lower racks of shopping carts.** Also look inside such items as trash cans, picnic chests, and toolboxes for merchandise customers may have "forgotten" to place on the checkout counter.

SUSPICIOUS SIGNALS—HOW TO SPOT POTENTIAL SHOPLIFTERS

If you know what to watch for, a large percentage of potential shoplifting acts can be prevented. Consider posting these guidelines in the store as reminders to employees. Take note of the following types of customers:

- Customers who spend more time watching you and your salespeople than they do looking at merchandise. Remember, before thieves can steal, they have to check to see if they're being observed.

- Customers who loiter, and handle a lot of merchandise, but make no apparent attempt to purchase.

- Shoppers who wear oversized and baggy clothing or who wear or carry overcoats or raincoats when the weather does not call for them.

- Customers who seem nervous or ill at ease and do not want any assistance.

- Customers who linger around counters located near exits. Many professional shoplifters "work the exits," where they can grab merchandise and get out quickly, usually to speed off in an automobile driven by an accomplice.

- People who carry large, empty, or nearly empty shopping bags or purses, especially those who walk around with their purses open. Also watch those who carry umbrellas (they are natural hiding places in the upside-down, partially open position).

- Customers who keep sending you away from the counter or from the department area to a back stockroom to check for other sizes, colors, or styles. Alert another salesperson or rapidly double back on them.

- Shoppers who walk around the store with large, unwrapped items—such as luggage or boxed merchandise—into which other items may be concealed.

- Customers who try to get behind sales counters or into back hallways or stockroom areas.

- Customers with baby carriages and strollers.

- Young people who come into the store in groups; juvenile shoplifting as the result of a dare or peer pressure is most likely among groups.

- Persons who create disturbances in the store; they may be part of a professional team. While everyone is attracted to the disturbance, other team members shoplift. Look around; see what is going on elsewhere.

- Very early, very late, or last-minute shoppers. Many professional shoplifters strike when sales personnel are preoccupied with their checking-in and checking-out duties.

- **Instruct all sales personnel to pause as they subtotal the sale.** At this point, look the customer directly in the eye and ask, "Is there anything else?" Pause until he or she responds. Interestingly, this is one of the most effective psychological deterrents to shoplifting and one of the easiest to implement. The number of items pulled from pockets and purses will be amazing.
- **Never leave a department or POS terminal unattended.** An unattended or understaffed department is an open invitation to steal. Employees should coordinate their breaks—even brief restroom breaks—so that someone is always on duty.

Merchandise Handling

- **Protect high-value merchandise.** When possible, keep it in locked storerooms, displaying only the samples. You can also use locked showcases or keep the highest value items (or the "most popular" items for thieves) behind staffed service counters. Never display expensive merchandise near exits. Also, despite their uninviting appearance—and the fact some customers find them off-putting or even offensive—chained and alarmed devices may have to be installed to protect some electronic equipment, appliances, expensive designer fashions, and fur coats.
- **Display merchandise neatly.** Organized displays make it easier to spot missing items. The same holds true for arranging and presenting countertop merchandise for customer examination and selection. Customers should be shown only one valuable item at a time. Beware of "switching," especially if you are in the jewelry trade. Professionals frequently attempt to switch your valuable diamonds or gemstones with their similarly mounted, cut-glass imitations. If possible, never turn your back on customers when getting merchandise for them.
- **Know the prices of your merchandise.** "Ticket switching" is a commonly used technique. Sales personnel should be instructed to double-check prices before ringing up any unusual "bargains." When possible, double-price all big-ticket items, especially those with easily switched string tags. Place the second price tag in an inconspicuous location, and inform all sales personnel to check these secondary pricing locations before recording the sale.
- **To deter ticket switching, use firmly attached plastic string tags, or price stickers that peel off in pieces if tampered with.** If tickets must be stapled on, use a distinctive stapling pattern recognizable to store personnel. When restocking merchandise, do not leave price stickers or tags lying about. You risk having some tickets pilfered by dishonest individuals and placed on much more expensive merchandise.
- **When possible, mark merchandise so it can be identified as store property.** Besides being vital in handling an apprehended shoplifter, such information can greatly increase the amount of merchandise recovered,

even in undiscovered thefts. Much stolen property recovered by police cannot be returned because it cannot be traced back to the stores from which it was stolen. Stamp items with a company logo or a coded serial number. Some types of high-value merchandise can also be marked with ultraviolet crayon or ink.

- **Don't use a pen or pencil to note the new price of sale or markdown merchandise on original sales tags.** You are openly inviting thieves to do likewise. Make new tickets or take the markdowns at the cash register.
- **Control fitting rooms.** This is an absolute must if you are in the retail clothing trade. If unattended, fitting rooms should be locked. An accurate count of the merchandise each customer takes into a fitting room should be made. The garments themselves should be closely observed to preclude, for example, the switching and concealing of an expensive dress for another that costs much less.

Store Layouts

- **Keep displays low enough so the sales staff can actually see the customers.** High fixtures, stacks of merchandise, and tall displays may look impressive—but they create protective screening and induce shoplifting.
- **Plan and coordinate the placement of POS terminals (cash registers) and customer service counters to maximize sales floor coverage.** Create as many "line-of-sight" settings as possible, and strive for "overlaps" where two or more employees can see the merchandise displays.
- **Try to arrange the store so everyone leaving must pass a checkout counter.**
- **Close and block off unused checkout aisles.**
- **Limit the number of exits.**
- **Depending on the nature and floor plan of the store, locate the manager's office where it will deter shoplifters (and dishonest employees).** If possible, build an elevated office, partially enclosed with opaque one-way glass, at the front of the store near the checkout register closest to the exit. From such a vantage point, you should be able to see the entire sales floor. Even when the office is unoccupied, the use of one-way glass will deter potential thieves—both customers and employees—who won't know whether or not they're being watched.

Deterrent Devices and Systems

- **Electronic sensing devices.** Great technological strides have been made in the development of electronic sensing devices to deter shoplifting. Radio frequency identification (RFID) tags and embedded sensors are among the most effective of the systems, but they are expensive and time-consuming to install and remove. In addition, they require close monitoring of the exit stations by trained sales or security personnel. Failure to remove or deactivate the sensors during the course of legitimate sales can annoy and embarrass honest customers and lead to false arrest or defamation of character lawsuits. Despite these drawbacks, if your store sells high-value items, you must consider the use of sensors as a part of the primary deterrent program.

- **Convex mirrors.** Strategically placed convex mirrors can help employees see around tall displays and into hard-to-see corners—but they allow wary shoplifters to keep an eye on employees, too. They also cause visual distortions that make it hard to accurately see what a potential shoplifter may be doing or concealing.

- **Flat mirrors.** The generous use of regular, flat mirrors mounted on pillars and walls is recommended. A long expanse of flat mirror mounted at the juncture of the rear wall and ceiling—and canted slightly downward—will provide excellent coverage of the entire sales floor in most small to medium-sized stores. Not only will such mirrors inhibit shoplifting, they can help supervisors monitor the actions of other store personnel.

- **Observation posts.** These utilize one-way mirrors and peepholes in offices, back rooms, and even in thick (but hollow) columns placed around a large store. They can be very effective in detecting shoplifters. Unfortunately, they're expensive to maintain because they must be staffed by someone at the observation post and by a colleague on the sales floor.

- **Closed-circuit television (CCTV) systems.** CCTV systems are less expensive than they used to be, but they still have the same cost drawback as observation posts, particularly in larger stores. Still, they can be very effective if properly maintained. Some store owners use "dummy" cameras to discourage shoplifters, but this subterfuge only works until the bogus nature of the cameras is discovered.

  If you intend to install a real CCTV system, be prepared to spend a significant amount of money to set it up and maintain it properly. Think carefully about where to place the monitoring portion of the system. Most such monitoring stations are located off the sales floor, in an office or back room.

  If shoplifting is a major problem, a glass-walled monitoring station can be constructed directly inside a main entrance so everyone can see it when they come into the store. Hook up a dozen or so CCTVs inside it, monitored by a uniformed security officer. Such an installation makes a tremendous visual impact and will definitely deter shoplifting, but it also destroys whatever dignified ambiance you may be striving to maintain within the store. It may even cause customer relations problems—because you have, in effect, created a war zone!

- **Uniformed guards.** The wisdom of using uniformed security guards in a store setting is debatable. Of course, their presence deters some shoplifting by juveniles and amateurs, but they will have little or no effect on the professionals. More likely, the guards' presence may lead to an increase in shoplifting because sales personnel (and even managers) are lulled into a false sense of security and become less observant of activities in their area of the sales floor—"that's what the guards are for." Uniformed guards are most effective when posted at exits. The best strategy, however, is to have a uniformed security staff work in conjunction with plainclothes guards and detectives.

The truth is, the best shoplifting deterrent in which a store owner can invest is an alert, well-trained staff. As part of the team effort, each store should develop a code of alerts using the store paging system or a similar communication method to summon supervisory or security personnel to a specific area whenever suspicious activity is observed. Such coding need not be elaborate, but it should quickly identify the department in which more coverage is needed. For example, a simple alerting system can be developed under the guise of announcing that a particular store employee (real or imaginary) "has a telephone call" on a particular "line number."

First, however, the sales area must be divided into sections, and each can be given a number that serves as its coded location marker. You might start numbering at the front left of the store and work your way across and down the length of store, ending in the right rear section. This numbered location grid then becomes the "telephone extension" of the coded announcement. See Figure 4-1 for an example of such a coded store layout.

If your store already has clearly defined department areas and each one has its own telephone extension number, the department's extension number may be used as an area identifier instead of laying out a grid.

Once the store has been sectioned off and coded, the system works this way:

- When a salesperson or the store manager (in the elevated office) notices suspicious activity in a particular department area, an announcement is made: "Mr. Seward, you have a telephone call on extension 105."

ACCESSORIES Ext. 1	SPORTSWEAR Ext. 2
DRESSES Ext. 3	SUITS & COATS Ext. 4
LINGERIE Ext. 5	SHOES Ext. 6

FIGURE 4-1 Antishoplifting grid.

- In this case, the fictitious "Mr. Seward" is the code word for a security problem and "105" designates the exact location where assistance is needed. The first digit signifies the first floor and "05" gives the specific location as noted on the store identity grid, or the telephone extension number of a specific department or area.
- Upon hearing the announcement, floor supervisors and other personnel move into the area to provide additional coverage.

CONFRONTING, DETAINING, AND ARRESTING SHOPLIFTERS

Now for the hard part: What do you do if you or one of your employees actually sees someone shoplift? The answer to that question brings into play a host of concerns, cautions, and legal caveats, all leading to one significant point: *Exercise extreme caution.*

First, bear in mind that *not everyone who removes merchandise from your store without paying for it is a thief.* The world is full of people who are senile, distraught, under the influence of adverse reactions from prescription drugs, mentally incompetent, preoccupied, or just plain absent-minded.

Many of these supposed "suspects" shop in your store, so do your best to evaluate the status and mental condition of anyone you confront as a suspected shoplifter, and *do not make an arrest or seek to prosecute if it does not appear warranted.* The adverse publicity for the store—as well as the possible civil judgments against the store if the case is lost—far outweigh any marginal benefits you might obtain from "seeking justice."

On the other hand, there are certainly customers who do shoplift with the intent to permanently deprive you of your goods. They are criminals, and you should strive to put them out of action. Prosecute everyone you catch, even first-time offenders—and they will *all* tell you that "this is their first time." Don't believe it! A strong and firm prosecution policy goes a long way toward establishing that your store is tough on crime—which is, in itself, an extremely effective deterrent.

The road that begins at the observing of an act of shoplifting and ends with a prosecution is not a smooth one; it is cratered with potholes, detours, breakdowns, and legal traps. As a store owner or manager, it is imperative that you learn to navigate this road.

Shoplifting Laws

Technically, shoplifting is considered a larceny, and while the laws vary from state to state and among local jurisdictions, they all contain a certain degree of commonality. In order to prove that a crime has been committed, two distinct elements must be present:

1. An act must have taken place that is prohibited by law—for example, the concealment of merchandise.
2. There must be *provable intent.* In a shoplifting case, this means you must be able to show, beyond any reasonable doubt, that the person detained *did not intend to pay* for the merchandise concealed.

Before a new store opens for business, it is wise to examine the shoplifting laws and any procedural guidelines that exist in your area. Consult with an attorney and local law enforcement agencies; check with the local district attorney, and so on. Many of these agencies have preprinted shoplifting guidelines on hand, and some have community or business liaison officers who can introduce programs to assist in training your staff. If the store is already in business and you're being considered for a management position, ask to see the written company policy about shoplifting and prosecution of thieves.

Confronting and Detaining Suspects

Before you confront or detain someone you suspect of shoplifting, the following requirements absolutely, positively must be met:

- You, or the employee accompanying you in detaining a suspect, must actually have seen the act of shoplifting take place.
- You, or that same employee, must have had the shoplifter *and the place of concealment* continuously in sight since the act occurred, and must be *absolutely certain* that the merchandise is still in the possession of the shoplifter.
- You must be certain the merchandise involved is, in fact, your store property.
- The individual must have demonstrated, by some overt act, that he or she does not intend to pay for the merchandise. Tearing off a price tag or concealing an item while still on the sales floor constitutes an act of shoplifting in most jurisdictions, but much stronger proof of "intent to permanently deprive" can be obtained by allowing the shoplifter to exit the store before making the apprehension.

If you are not positive about all these issues—that is, if there is even the slightest doubt in your mind—do not stop the person. Also do not, under any circumstances, make the stop if the individual, or even that portion of the individual where the merchandise was being concealed (a purse, a box, a stroller), has been out of your (or your employee's) constant line of sight, even if only for seconds. The bottom line: *Legally, you are far better off losing the merchandise than being faced with a civil suit if you make the detention and then, belatedly, discover your suspected shoplifter is "clean."*

There are two primary reasons you can end up with a clean shoplifter:

1. They frequently realize or sense when they have been observed, and manage to get rid of the merchandise before being confronted.
2. Some, as pointed out earlier, surreptitiously pass the merchandise off to accomplices, then initiate false arrest legal action against you (depending on your comments and actions at the time of the confrontation).

It is important to note that the term "false arrest" does not pertain solely to actions by police officers. Once you stop and detain someone—that is, prevent the person from engaging in normal activities—you have, technically, made a "citizen's arrest." So before you act, be sure, be careful, and be professional.

The entire issue of confronting and detaining suspected shoplifters is, unfortunately, often misunderstood. Unless you can fully and correctly explain it, you could easily wind up with a very disgruntled and frustrated sales staff. On its face, it doesn't make much sense that well-meaning employees can take no action if, after they observe an act of shoplifting, they "break contact" to report the theft instead of keeping the suspect continuously in sight. This is where proper training comes in for both supervisory and general sales personnel—and it cannot be overemphasized.

Arresting Shoplifters

If you are certain that all the previously mentioned requirements have been met, you may then proceed with a detention and, if warranted, subsequent arrest. As a general rule, train all employees to follow the guidelines in Figure 4-2. Consider posting these guidelines in the back of the store, as a reminder to employees.

Interviewing Suspects

For the most part, interviewing suspected shoplifters is not that difficult—either they have your merchandise or they don't. If you did not recover the goods at the time you apprehended the person, or are not positive they currently have it in their possession, you should not have made the stop or be interviewing them. On the other hand, if you recovered the merchandise or are positive they still have it (and that you can obtain it by request or by conducting a lawful search), you have direct, **prima facie evidence** of the crime. Actually, in such cases, a lengthy interview and written admission of guilt, while desirable, is not absolutely necessary. As long as you have the evidence, the witnesses, and the identity of the shoplifter, you can obtain an arrest warrant.

- **Be careful!!! Not all shoplifters react quietly to being arrested.** Many of them, especially professionals and substance abusers, can become violent and may carry firearms or other weapons. Many work with accomplices who will come to their aid if they're detained. *If you do not feel you can physically handle the situation, do not attempt the arrest.* Instead, get descriptions, vehicle identification data, and direction of travel, and immediately notify your local police.

- **If you do decide to physically restrain someone and they resist,** you can use only the minimum amount of force necessary to overcome that resistance. When possible, have someone call the police before the actual apprehension takes place. Officers may be able to respond in time to provide assistance.

- **Try to have a witness to the shoplifting and, especially, to the detention.** Not only will this second person be able to help safeguard your personal safety, he or she will be in a position to hear any admissions made by the suspect, or be a witness in the store's defense if your "clean" shoplifter files a false arrest lawsuit.

- **Do not accuse the shoplifter of stealing or indicate that a "mistake" may have been made.** You may find you are wrong on both counts. Approach in a confident manner, identify yourself, and firmly state, "I believe you have some merchandise that you have forgotten to pay for. Would you return to the store with me, please?" Without waiting for a response, escort the suspect back into the store. Recover the merchandise before returning to the store, when possible. Note and remember where it was concealed.

- **Once you are back in the store, take the suspect to an office or private area.** If someone has not already done so, call the police. If you are fortunate, they will be able to respond and take over. They will conduct whatever interviews and interrogations are necessary, take written statements, and take custody of the evidence. If, unfortunately, the police, for any number of very valid reasons, cannot respond in a reasonable amount of time or, as a matter of department policy, do not investigate shoplifting incidents, you will have to make a decision as to whether to interview the suspect yourself.

FIGURE 4-2 Guidelines for arresting shoplifting suspects.

Getting the evidence and the true identity of the shoplifter, however, usually requires an interview. And there are other good reasons for interviewing shoplifting suspects, including the following:

- To obtain an admission of guilt.
- To obtain a written, signed confession.
- To determine whether the suspect has other store merchandise on his or her person or in a vehicle, residence, or other location.
- To determine the identities of any accomplices.
- To learn more about the shoplifting techniques, so that existing anti-shoplifting procedures can be reviewed and enhanced if necessary.
- To have the suspect sign a form releasing you and others from civil liability resulting from the detention and interrogation. (More on this subject later.)

Now that you have a better understanding of *why* you should conduct the interview, let's go over some basic procedural guidelines for *how* to do it. Figure 4-3 provides a checklist. Again, consider posting these guidelines in a back room of the store, or in the location to which you take suspected shoplifters, to remind employees of proper interviewing procedures.

After the preliminary interview—which involves determining the identity of the person and what they tried to steal—your interview goal is twofold: (1) to obtain an oral admission of guilt in the presence of a witness and (2) to obtain sufficient related information that can be used to prepare a subsequent written statement. The interview and the statement need not be lengthy or elaborate—in fact, it's best if they are not. Keep in mind that any admission of guilt, oral or written, obtained by the use of intimidation, threat, coercion, or promise of any kind will be inadmissible in court and could leave you and the store vulnerable for civil liability. You must be able to demonstrate that all such admissions are voluntary, which is another good reason to have a witness present.

Conduct the interview and obtain the necessary details in an orderly and logical manner. Make notes as you go along (your witness can perform this function). At the very least, you must obtain the following information and include it in a written statement:

- Date
- Location (city, state)
- Name and location of the store
- Full identity and address of the shoplifter
- Time of the offense
- Description of each item taken, including its value
- Method used by the shoplifter to conceal the merchandise
- Admission that the merchandise was taken without any intention of payment

- Identify yourself to the suspect.

- Take the suspect to an office or similar private area.

- Have another person present. If the suspected shoplifter is a female, your witness should also be a female.

- Recover the merchandise if it was not obtained during the detention, watching carefully to ensure the suspect does not discard it while being returned to the store. State the item(s) stolen and the place of concealment. This will usually convince the shoplifter that he or she has been caught red-handed. If it does not, courts have held that if you have "reasonable cause" to believe the suspect has your merchandise, you may legally conduct a search to recover it.

- Instruct the shoplifter to place on a desk or table all items he or she did not pay for. There may be other merchandise of which you are not aware.

- Do not make any threats—and do not make any promises.

- If you have decided to go ahead with the arrest, do not accept any payment for the merchandise.

- Obtain the full identification of the shoplifter, cross-checking it with documentation in his or her possession. Attempt to obtain identification cards with photographs and physical descriptions and compare them with your suspect. Many professional shoplifters carry false or stolen identification documents.

FIGURE 4-3 Guidelines for interviewing suspected shoplifters.

With the interview concluded and (presumably) an admission of guilt obtained, the next step is to have the shoplifter execute and sign a written statement. Figure 4-4 provides a sample of a standard statement form. Although it is best to get a statement in the shoplifter's own handwriting, it is not absolutely necessary. The written statement, while serving as a valid form of confession, also is an excellent vehicle for performing several other functions. In addition to including the specific issues itemized previously, follow these guidelines when obtaining a written statement from a shoplifter:

- **Make sure the statement includes a paragraph that confirms the voluntary nature of the statement.** It can simply state: "I hereby offer this statement, voluntarily and of my own free will, without having been subjected to any threats, unlawful inducements, or promises of reward or immunity."

- **If applicable, obtain a consent to search release.** If it is determined during the interview that the shoplifter has, in his or her automobile or home, other items stolen from the store, a comment giving permission for a search

FIGURE 4-4 Sample of standard statement form.

STATEMENT

Date: _____ Time: _____

Location: _____

City/County of: _____ State: _____

I, _____, state that before I was questioned by _____ he/she identified himself/herself to me as _____

    I hereby offer this statement, voluntarily and of my own free will without having been subjected to any threats, unlawful inducements, or promises of reward or immunity.

_____
_____
_____
_____
_____
_____
_____
_____
_____
_____
_____
_____

Page __1__ of __3__

and recovery of such items should be included in the statement. A separate, voluntary "Consent to Search" form can also be used (see Figure 4-5).

Professional security officers frequently do not apprehend shoplifters until they have reached their automobiles. By delaying the apprehension, these officers have found that they were able to recover additional merchandise that had been stolen by brazen shoplifters who had made more than one trip into the store. A word of caution, however; shoplifters frequently work in groups. Do not follow someone out to a remote parking lot where you could be "ganged up on" and attacked.

■ **Include a standard paragraph that absolves you and the store from civil liability charges in case an error has been made and no offense has been committed.** The phrasing can be something like: "I hereby release the person or persons who detained me in connection with the aforesaid incident and his or her principals, employees, and customers from any claim or demand arising out of or in connection with said incident."

FIGURE 4-5 Sample of voluntary consent to search form.

VOLUNTARY CONSENT TO SEARCH

I, _____, have been informed of my constitutional right not to have a search made of the premises hereinafter described without a search warrant, and of my right to refuse to consent to such a search.

I hereby voluntarily waive such rights without having been subjected to any threats, unlawful inducements, or promises of reward or immunity, and grant permission to _____ _____ and _____ to enter and conduct a complete search of my premises located at _____ _____

(or, my vehicle, which is fully identified as follows: _____ _____).

The above named persons are hereby authorized to seize and recover all such stolen property as they may discover. Further, I state that I will make no claim against the above named persons, the ___(Name of business)___, its officers and employees, in connection with any legal suit or demand arising as a result of this search.

_____
Signature

_____
_____
_____
Address

Witnesses: (Name, Title, Address)

_____
_____

Continued

You can also use a separate form, referred to as a "Civil Release," as shown in Figure 4-6. Before using a Civil Release form, clear it with the store's attorney and the local prosecuting attorney to ensure that the format meets the pertinent laws in your area.

- **Make sure you have all necessary signatures.** These include:

  ◇ The signature and address of the shoplifter
  ◇ Your signature, position, and address
  ◇ The signature, position, and address of the witness

FIGURE 4-5 *(Continued)*

Statement of _____
(Continued)

A. Consent to search and recover other stolen store property.

I also admit to having the following additional stolen store property:

_____

_____

_____

_____

_____

It is located at: _____

_____

I hereby voluntarily grant permission for _____ *to enter the location described above and seize and recover all property described above.*

B. Civil Release

I hereby release the person or persons who detained me in connection with the aforesaid incident and his or her principals, employees and customers from any claim or demand arising out of or in connection with this incident.

Page _2_ of _3_

Continued

◇ In the event the shoplifter declines to sign the statement after it has been prepared, make a note on it to that effect, sign and date it, and have the witness sign it.

- **Call the police.** After the statement has been obtained, notify local police (if they have not already been summoned) and give them the details of the offense. As a general rule, they will take custody of the shoplifter. The person who witnessed the act of shoplifting will be required to appear before a magistrate and swear to and sign the warrant for arrest. Read the warrant carefully to ensure that it is correct. *Never sign a blank warrant.*
- **Prepare a record of the incident.** While the events are still fresh in everyone's mind, brief, written statements of the entire incident should be made by everyone involved in the observation, apprehension, and interviewing

FIGURE 4-5 (*Continued*)

Statement of _____ (Continued)

I have read this entire statement which consists of _____ pages. I have initialed each page and each correction. I fully understand this statement and it is true, accurate and complete to the best of my knowledge and belief.

_____
Signature

_____
_____
Address

_____
Signature of person obtaining statement

_____
_____
_____
Position and address

_____
Signature of witness

_____
_____
Position and address

Page __3__ of __3__

of the shoplifter. Depending on the role played, these statements (and sometimes, sketches) should include the following details:

◇ The date, time, and location within the store
◇ The role and/or employment position of the witness
◇ A complete description of the shoplifter, plus that of any accomplices
◇ A description of the merchandise taken
◇ The method(s) used by the shoplifter to steal the merchandise
◇ The general pattern of the activities of the shoplifter while in the store

FIGURE 4-6 Sample of civil release form.

CIVIL RELEASE

I, ______________________________________, of __________
(Address) ______, for valuable and sufficient consideration of forbearance of Prosecution running to and received by me, do hereby release and forever discharge individually and severally the employees, directors, and stockholders of the ______________
(Name of business) ______ from any and all demands, claims, or causes of action whatsoever which I may now have, may have had, or may have in the future by reason of, or in any matter related to my __________ (Detention, Arrest, Discharge) __________
________ for ______________________________________

____

_____ at __________ (Location) __________ on ______________, and I hereby waive all right, title, and interest in property surrendered in connection with the aforementioned charge.

____
Signature

____
Date

Witnesses: (Name, Position, Address)

____

____

____

- ◇ The point of exit from the store
- ◇ The place of apprehension and the identity of those involved
- ◇ Comments made by the shoplifter at the time of the apprehension
- ◇ Comments made by the shoplifter during the interview, with emphasis on admissions of guilt

These statements should then be signed, dated, and filed in a safe place. They may be used to refresh memories when testimonies are given at a subsequent trial of the shoplifter.

Juvenile Shoplifters

Almost one-third of shoplifters who are arrested are juveniles, persons under the age of 18.[3] Underage shoplifting poses special problems, and the procedures for detaining juveniles are different than those used for adults. Instead of an arrest warrant, for example, a criminal complaint against a child is made on a different form, called a **juvenile petition**.

Each local jurisdiction has its own procedures for the handling of juvenile shoplifters, and every store employee should know them. Some police departments want to be notified of every such apprehension, because it helps them become aware of repeat offenders and may help the store decide whether to prosecute. Other police departments don't want to be notified unless parents are uncooperative and legal action is desired. Still others take a middle stance—they'll come to the store and take the offender home to his or her parents, or perhaps call parents to the store, but they don't seem to take kids' shoplifting very seriously.

In short, it is up to the local store owner or manager to find out how law enforcement handles these incidents. Agree on the rules, and train your employees to follow them.

CARE AND CONTROL OF SHOPLIFTING EVIDENCE

Many shoplifting cases have been lost in court because the evidence—that is, the merchandise stolen—was lost, improperly safeguarded, or not retained (for example, returned to inventory and sold). To obtain a successful shoplifting prosecution, the store must be able to demonstrate that an intact *chain of custody* has existed from the time the merchandise in question was retrieved from the shoplifter until presented in court.

Therefore, one of the first things to do after an arrest is to mark the merchandise recovered. This should be done by the person who witnessed the shoplifting incident—the one who will appear as the complainant against the shoplifter in court. That person should initial and date each piece of merchandise recovered, preferably right on the merchandise itself, not on a tag that could be torn off.

A special evidence tag can be affixed to the merchandise for this purpose. Place the marked merchandise in a sealed bag or box, and have the complainant—again, the store employee who will represent the store in court—initial it. The bag or box should be marked to indicate the date, the name of the store, and the identity of the person apprehended, and can then be stored in a safe place until the trial. This evidence must be brought to court by the complainant. Examples of an evidence tag and a form that can be used to mark and identify the sealed box or bag of evidence are shown in Figure 4-7.

In many cases, the police officers who take custody of the shoplifter also take custody of the evidence. If that is standard procedure in your locality, make sure you get an itemized receipt for all of the merchandise released and store it in a safe place until the trial. After the trial is over, you will need the receipt to get the merchandise back.

FIGURE 4-7 Sample of evidence tag and seal for stolen merchandise.

EVIDENCE TAG

Description: _____

Received/Seized from: _____

Received by: _____

Date Obtained: _____ Time: _____

Offense: _____

CHAIN OF CUSTODY

Date	From	To

Print Name _____   Print Name _____

Signature _____   Signature _____

Purpose of Transfer _____

Date	From	To

Print Name _____   Print Name _____

Signature _____   Signature _____

Purpose of Transfer _____

Date	From	To

Print Name _____   Print Name _____

Signature _____   Signature _____

Purpose of Transfer _____

EVIDENCE SEAL

Location: _____

Owner/Victim: _____

Name of Suspect: _____

Offense: _____

Comment: _____

_____

All evidence contained herein has been identified, initialed, and recorded on Evidence Tags. I have sealed the container and have initialed the seal.

Date _____   _____

                               Signature

                               _____

                               _____

                               Position and Address

BOX/BAG _____ of _____.

EVIDENCE

If the police do not take the evidence, it will be up to you to safeguard it. *Do not return it to stock.*

COURT APPEARANCES

Once you (the complainant) have pressed criminal charges against a shoplifter, you will often be required to appear in court that same day or the following morning. Rarely will the case actually "go to trial" at that time, but be prepared by bringing the evidence with you. As a general rule, you will receive, at a later date, notification or a subpoena that states the specific date and time you are to be in court.

Make sure every witness who receives a subpoena gets to the trial on time and understands that all testimony given in court must be accurate, impartial, nonprejudicial, and truthful. Cases have been lost, and civil suits for false arrest filed, because complainants and witnesses failed to appear in court—or presented inaccurate, biased, and/or untruthful testimony.

If there are unusual or extenuating circumstances in the case, it's a good idea to arrive at the court well before the trial starts to discuss the situation with the prosecuting attorney.

Discussion of Shoplifting Incidents

While it is understandable—and tempting—it is best not to discuss shoplifting incidents among fellow workers, especially before they are brought to trial. Casual remarks ("I just knew she was a thief") could be overheard by someone who knows the person about whom the remark was made, and in this litigious society, this could result in a civil suit against you for defamation of character. Once a person has been formally charged with an offense, the incident should not be discussed with anyone except involved store personnel, the police, and the prosecuting attorney.

Dropping Charges

Occasionally, after formal charges have been made, mitigating circumstances may arise that prompt a decision not to prosecute the alleged shoplifter. A decision to drop charges (called **nolle prosse** or *nolle prosequi* in legal terms) is usually recommended by the local prosecuting attorney, but it is still ultimately your decision—and charges cannot be dropped without your approval.

If you agree with the decision to drop the charges, a Civil Release form must be signed, in the presence of the prosecuting attorney, by the person arrested. Similar to the form shown in Figure 4-6, this is the individual's agreement not to file a civil suit against you or the store for the arrest or detention. Make sure you receive a copy of this signed Civil Release and store it in a safe place.

SHOPLIFTING PREVENTION CHECKLIST

❏ Train employees to prevent shoplifting rather than watch it occur.

❏ Design the store layout in such a manner as to deter shoplifting.

❏ Arrange the fixtures in the store to provide line-of-sight coverage of potential shoplifters.

❏ Make sure all high-value merchandise is properly protected.

❏ Double-price all expensive items, with the secondary marking located in a hidden position.

❏ Use deterrent devices and systems such as locks, alarms, mirrors, and electronic sensors.

❏ Implement a "shoplifter alert" notification plan.

❏ Make sure employees are knowledgeable about suspicious behavior and shoplifting methods.

❏ Train all employees in proper antishoplifting customer relations.

❏ Train all store employees (especially managers and supervisors) in proper procedures for confronting, detaining, and arresting suspected shoplifters.

❏ Coordinate your program and policies with local laws and police procedures.

❏ Develop and implement special policies for handling juvenile shoplifters.

❏ Make sure all store managers know how to properly handle shoplifting evidence, court appearances, and dropping charges.

❏ Incorporate all shoplifting prevention policies into the store's written operations manual.

CHAPTER SUMMARY

Even after all the antishoplifting care that is taken by retailers, less than 20 percent of these thieves are arrested. This chapter chronicled many suggestions for preventing shoplifting that should be made part of any retailer's employee training program. They included recognizing suspicious behavior and the following major points:

- **Shoplifting methods.** There are three primary methods: sleight-of-hand, devices, and distraction. The latter method also includes so-called "clean" shoplifters who pretend to steal, then file lawsuits against the store for false arrest or defamation.

- **Preventive measures.** The goal is prevention, not apprehension. Train and motivate your sales staff to this end. Develop a reputation as a "tight store." Use shoplifting deterrent devices, psychological procedures and barriers, and store layout strategies to accomplish this, including customer relations tactics, merchandise handling procedures, and store designs that preempt and/or discourage shoplifting.
- **Confronting, detaining, and arresting shoplifters.** Exercise extreme caution at all times. There are both physical and legal dangers to consider every time you or one of your employees detects a suspected shoplifter—and must decide whether to confront, detain, and/or make an arrest. Make sure there is someone on the sales floor at all times who is familiar with the shoplifting laws in your area, and your company's detention procedures both for adults and juveniles.
- **When to "let 'em go."** Be sure at least one employee saw the larceny take place, that the shoplifter still has possession of the merchandise when confronted, and that the person has clearly demonstrated an intent to not pay for the merchandise in question. Don't hesitate to let a shoplifter go if you are not sure of these things. When you do apprehend a suspect, be professional and courteous at all times, making no threats or promises. Follow your preestablished procedures, which should include very specific instructions for dealing with juveniles.
- **Precautions for a solid court case.** Don't lose a shoplifting case because the evidence was inadvertently mishandled. Attend the hearings on time, and realize you are representing the store and the retail industry. Be professional, don't exaggerate the truth, and don't gossip about the case with coworkers.

DISCUSSION QUESTIONS

1. Why is it hard to stop shoplifting? Research what courts in your area, or elsewhere in the country, are doing about this type of crime, and write a short report about a program or sentencing idea that seems to be working.
2. Describe the three main shoplifting methods and give examples of each.
3. Why can it cost a merchant less to let a shoplifter go than stop one who turns out to be "clean?"
4. What are the most important things to keep in mind when deciding whether or not to confront a shoplifter? How important is it that the person leaves the store before being confronted?
5. Research and list the most common items stolen by shoplifters. Do juveniles target different types of merchandise than adults?
6. Most shoplifters who are arrested are men. Does this mean most

shoplifters are men—or that women just get away with it more often? What do you think?

7. As a store owner, how would you balance the need to be known as a "tight store" with a friendly ambience that makes honest, legitimate customers feel welcome?

8. How are many "solid" shoplifting cases lost at trial? Find out more about the statistics in your market, and any loopholes that shoplifters may use to avoid prosecution in your area.

ENDNOTES

1. "Crime in the U.S.," Federal Bureau of Investigation, Washington, D.C., 2002.
2. Joe Kleinsasser, "Minor Offense Has Major Economic Implications," *Inside WSU* (newsletter of Wichita State University), Wichita, Kansas, September 21, 2000.
3. "Crime in the U.S.," Federal Bureau of Investigation, Washington, D.C., 2002.

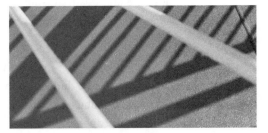

5

ARMED
ROBBERY

P olice in Vallejo, California, said the young man hired by a Toys 'R Us store in December 2004 had been making plans to rob the store "for some time." In May of 2005, he and two armed accomplices broke into the store after closing and tied up the few workers who happened to still be on the premises, but not before they managed to alert police. In the getaway attempt, two of the suspects were apprehended, but the former employee fled the scene, attempted a carjacking, and was shot and killed by police.[1]

This incident is only one of thousands of armed robberies of retail stores in the United States every year. This chapter examines ways to control risk and loss from what is potentially the most dangerous situation you and your employees may face in the course of a business day.

Of course, the first and most obvious reason armed robberies are dangerous is the involvement of a weapon—or at least, a robber's threat that he or she is armed. Second, the robber usually has no weapons training or experience and is often either under the influence of alcohol or drugs or is frantic as an addict who lacks them. Finally, unlike shoplifting, you cannot choose the time, place, and manner in which to confront the perpetrators (or not). Instead, you and your employees face a life-and-death situation in which the *correct* split-second decisions must be made. Specific subject areas covered in this chapter include:

- Key safety and security issues
- Pre-robbery preparations
- What to do during a robbery
- Post-robbery actions
- Court appearances

By definition, robbery is the taking of property of another by force or the threat of force. Unlike burglary, which generally involves breaking into premises when no one is around, robbery is a personal, face-to-face confrontation that is frightening and traumatic. But though armed robbery is perhaps the most potentially dangerous situation you may face as a retailer, it is important to understand that the inherent risks can be controlled—from both a personal and a financial standpoint.

KEY SAFETY AND SECURITY ISSUES

First and foremost, everyone in the store must understand that *it is foolhardy to argue with a gun.* Store management's training efforts should be directed at controlling and reducing vulnerability to armed robberies, and minimizing the financial loss if robbery occurs—not trying to stop a robbery in progress.

Second, whether you're an employee, manager, or owner, accept the fact that you have no control over someone who bursts into the store brandishing a weapon, demanding money—but you *do* have control over certain other aspects of the crime. You *can* control the amount of the loss. You *can* create policies that reduce the danger of personal injury to yourself and fellow employees, and aid in the apprehension and conviction of the perpetrator. In short, there are actions you can take before, during, and after an armed robbery that will make the best of a very unpleasant and dangerous situation.

BEFORE A ROBBERY OCCURS

Alertness, knowledge, proper training, and effective cash management can minimize—and in some cases, prevent—losses from armed robbery.

As discussed in Chapter 1, you should be highly alert and exercise extreme caution when opening and closing a store or making a bank deposit. Resist the danger of getting into habits, doing things the same way at the same times, day after day. Your risk of being held up at those times is very high, particularly if you don't use the risk minimization strategies and tactics described in this book.

If you carry high-value merchandise such as jewelry or electronic equipment, or if your store is large enough to generate large amounts of cash, you will attract professional robbers who know how to control themselves, their weapons, and the situation, at least to a large extent. These career criminals are well organized and can be ruthless.

Perhaps unfortunately, however, as a retailer you are more likely to be confronted by the much more dangerous "semiprofessional" or "amateur" robbers. They may be opportunists, thrill seekers who are absolutely new at holdups. They may be unstable, unpredictable characters: substance abusers, juveniles, young men seeking to make a name for themselves, or desperate individuals who see robbery as the only solution to pressing financial problems. They are almost all nervous, easily excitable, and subject to losing control—of themselves, their weapons, and the situation—often with tragic results. Treat them as cautiously as you would a hand grenade or a loaded gun.

Be sure all employees learn and discuss the information in this chapter. If they do, the chances of you or a coworker being injured or killed by an armed robber will be reduced, and the store may also limit its financial losses.

Pre-Robbery Guidelines

Here are some primary pre-robbery guidelines to learn, understand, and follow:

- **Be alert at all times to what is going on around you.** Watch for individuals in or around the store who act suspiciously. What is "suspicious" behavior? You really will notice it—people who seem to be watching the employees or security cameras more than shopping, the person who comes in just to get change without buying anything, or people who ask a lot of questions but seem preoccupied. Be especially watchful if, in addition to a suspicious person inside, you can see someone else sitting outside in a vehicle. Increase your vigilance just before closing time, when there may be only a few customers in the store and your employees are

OUT OF THE MOUTHS OF BABES: FORMULA THIEVES AT WORK

Shoplifters are not always kids palming candy or homeless people trying to make ends meet. Some are members of well-organized crime rings that target certain types of merchandise. One of the most profitable and oft-stolen items is baby formula. A sampling of cases from 2004 to 2005:

- In Oklahoma, four Mexican nationals were charged with larceny and concealment of stolen property in a theft ring that investigators say was shipping about 2,000 pounds of formula per week from Oklahoma to Kentucky. A cache of formula, stolen a few cans at a time from supermarkets and convenience stores, was discovered in a rented storage unit.

- In Tennessee, two routine traffic stops prompted the seizure of more than 4,500 cans of stolen formula.

- In North Carolina, seven Honduran immigrants were sentenced and deported for their roles in a theft ring that specialized in over-the-counter drugs and baby food, worth about $14 million.

Law enforcement officials say the powdered infant formula is used to cut illegal drugs, or is re-labeled and sold on the black market at deeply discounted prices. Stores are fighting back by stocking only small amounts of formula on their shelves, installing video surveillance cameras in baby product aisles, putting it behind counters, and/or locking it up.

Source: Michael Rubinkam, "Protecting Store Assets: Securing Often-Targeted Baby Formula," June 7, 2005, and "Oklahoma Authorities Break Shoplifting Ring," June 2, 2005, Associated Press, on www.SecurityWatchInfo.com, Cygnus Business Media, Fort Atkinson, Wisconsin.

engaged in closeout activities. If something—anything—doesn't seem right, don't hesitate to call your local police.

- **Implement logical cash management policies.** Obviously, the less cash there is on hand for a robber to take, the smaller the store's loss will be, so don't allow large amounts of cash to accumulate in the registers or in the store's safe. Make bank deposits every day. If it's unsafe or impractical to leave the store and make the deposits yourself, look into using an armored car company.

- **Make frequent cash "pulls" from the registers.** Don't let the registers or POS terminals accumulate large amounts of cash. This is especially important for **cash wraps** (checkout stands) located near exits, which are frequently the targets of "snatch-and-run" specialists as well as armed robbers. Instruct cashiers to keep large-denomination currency under the tray in the cash drawer rather than in plain view. When you make periodic cash pickups from a register, count the money with the salesperson responsible

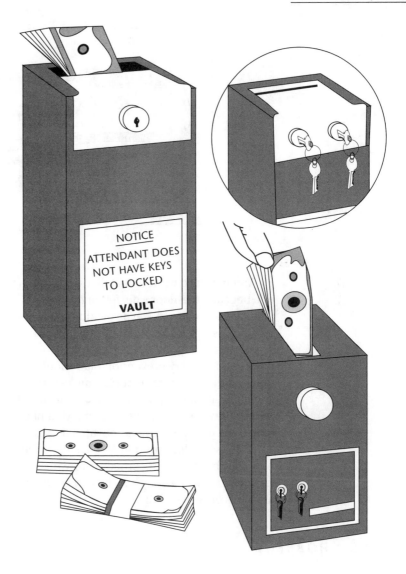

Figure 5-1 Drop boxes and slot safes.

for it, and provide a signed receipt for the amount taken. This will help in closing out the register at the end of the business day or shift, as well as in discouraging "shortage reportage" by a dishonest or careless cashier.

■ **Install drop boxes or slot safes.** These can effectively reduce cash losses due to robbery because they are usually bolted to countertops or floors and have signs saying they can't be opened by the employee on duty—which is true. They can't! If you decide to get one, however, be sure it's properly made and installed. (Also check whether some type of baffle or mechanism behind the slot prevents dishonest employees from "fishing" for the money envelopes inside.) Figure 5-1 shows examples of cash repositories.

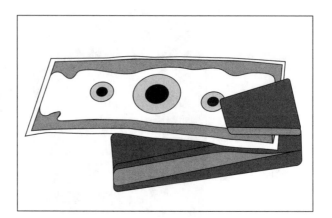

Figure 5-2 Wireless money trap.

You may also want to install a **secondary repository**, such as a wall safe or a beneath-the-floor safe, for large amounts of money or exceptional valuables. If you believe this type of additional safe is warranted, have it installed when the store is closed and do not mention its existence to general store employees.

A good robbery prevention plan should also include some of the various types of alarm and camera systems described in Chapter 3. Another alarm known as a "**money trap**" is also available for use in cash registers and money drawers. It is designed somewhat like a clip, and when the money is pulled out of it, an alarm is activated. Figure 5-2 shows this type of device.

The use of "**bait money**"—packets of paper currency with serial numbers that have been recorded or in which explosive vials of indelible inks have been placed—may also be considered if the store typically keeps large amounts of cash on hand.

DURING A ROBBERY

This is a dangerous time. As the store manager, if at all possible, you should try to take the lead in controlling the situation as best you can.

Absolutely do not confront the robber(s). Even if you do not see the weapons they claim to have, you must operate as though they absolutely are armed and willing to use them. In fact, if the robbers are confronted or frustrated in their efforts to rob the store, they are more likely to use force. Accordingly, your risk of injury or death is far greater when you confront an armed robber than it is when you confront a shoplifter. Some law enforcement experts say it is unwise even to make confrontational eye contact with a robber, so remain alert and observant, but don't glare or scowl.

Communicate with the robber(s). If you can establish a relationship (even an adversarial one) with a robber, other employees and customers alike become incidental players and thus are less likely to be harmed. Such action on your part can help defuse the highly charged and hazardous initial period of confrontation when the robber is trying to establish control.

Cooperate, but do not volunteer. Try to remain calm. Obey the robber's commands, and instruct everyone else to do the same. However, do not voluntarily remove cash from or reveal the location of any secondary or concealed money repositories. If you are asked to stuff money or items into a bag, put the smallest bills in first, and remember, "stuffing" haphazardly means the bag fills more quickly—with less cash.

Do not take risks. People who are not directly involved in the holdup should keep away rather than try to intervene and risk making the robber more nervous. Control your movements carefully, and don't reach for anything—a drawer, a pocket, a purse—without explaining first to the robber exactly what you are going to do.

Collect evidence. If a note is presented, do not give it back unless it is asked for. Drop it in the register or safe or set it aside. The fingerprints and writing on it could be valuable evidence for the police. If you see the robber put an ungloved hand on any surface, note its location so it can be "dusted" later for fingerprints.

Pay attention. The best thing you can do during a robbery is to be incredibly observant. Detailed physical descriptions, including the robber's manner of dress, speech, and distinctive characteristics (tattoos, scars, and so on), are among the most important items of information you can give to the police.

AFTER A ROBBERY

The first thing to do after the robber leaves your store—that is, if it can be done without endangering yourself or others—is see which way the robber went, at what speed, and so on. If a getaway vehicle was used, try to note the make and model, license number, color, damage, and/or any other distinct characteristics. Remember, though, that today's robbers are sometimes on bicycles or even on foot, losing themselves in a busy neighborhood and/or sauntering along like nothing happened so as not to call attention to themselves.

Second, *call the police* (unless someone was able to activate a silent holdup alarm or surreptitiously make a telephone call while the robbery was

Figure 5-3 Sample form for reporting a robbery.

INCIDENT REPORT FORM

Date and Time of Incident: _____

Location of Incident: _____

Type of Incident: _____

Report Made by: _____

Brief Description of Incident

_____

_____

_____

Description of Suspect(s) *(Use separate form for each)*

General: Sex _____ Race _____ Age _____ Height _____ Weight _____

                Scars/Marks _____ Other _____

Hair: Color _____ Length _____ Style _____

Face: Type _____ Complexion _____ Mustache/Beard _____

Voice: Pitch _____ Accent _____ Impediment _____

Clothing: Describe–top to bottom _____

                _____

Mask: Type _____ Color _____

Weapon: Describe–Gun _____ Knife _____

                _____

Names: Unknown _____ Known _____

                Called other suspects by name: _____

Items Taken

Money: Amount Bills _____ Amount Coins _____ Other _____

                Total Monetary Loss: _____

Merchandise: Description and Value *(Use reverse if necessary)* _____

                _____

Manner of Escape

On Foot _____ By Vehicle _____ Other _____

Vehicle Description: Make _____ Color _____ Model _____ Year _____

License No. _____ Condition _____

Direction of Escape _____

_____

                                      Signature

in progress). Be sure to begin by saying, "There has been an armed robbery," and be sure to mention whether or not people have been injured. You will probably speak to a dispatcher who will, in turn, relay your information to a patrol car and the appropriate emergency medical personnel. *Stay on the line until all necessary information is transmitted.* If in the excitement of the moment you hang up too soon, the police may be delayed in getting to your store or, worse, may unknowingly pass the escaping robbers while en route to the scene because, in your haste, you hung up before describing their vehicle.

Third, do whatever you can to *assist employees or customers* who may be in shock or have suffered injuries until ambulances arrive.

Fourth, *preserve the evidence.* Get the rope or clothesline from your emergency kit and cordon off the entire area until the police arrive and complete their investigation. Protect anything the robber may have touched—the cash register, the countertop, merchandise, even the entry and exit door handles—anything may bear latent fingerprints of the suspects. If shots were fired and shell casings were ejected, leave them exactly where they fell.

Fifth, *write down your description of the robber(s) as soon as possible* after the robbery, and have all other witnesses do the same. Be sure they write these descriptions separately, *without comparing notes*. The descriptions should include the following:

- General physical characteristics—gender, race, age, height, weight, and build—with special notation of any disabilities, scars, marks, tattoos, or other unique identifying features
- Hair (color, length, style)
- Face (shape, complexion, mustache, beard, glasses)
- Voice (high, low, accent, speech impediment)
- Names, if more than one robber and they addressed each other by name
- Hands (rough, smooth, rings, wristwatches, gloves)
- Clothing (describe fully, top to bottom, hat or mask to shoes)
- Weapons (type, color, where concealed)

An example of a standard incident report form suitable for prompting good, thorough descriptions of the suspect(s) is shown in Figure 5-3.

COURT APPEARANCES

The store owner is the person typically required to be the complainant, the party who presses criminal charges against an armed robber; or the local prosecuting attorney may do it on your behalf. Either way, you may be required to appear in court at arraignments or hearings before the actual trial. Generally, you will receive notification or a **subpoena** that states the specific date and time you are to be in court.

WORTH NOTING: INTERESTING RETAIL ROBBERY COURT CASES

- In November 2002, a man entered a retail shoe store, concealed a pair of boots inside his pants, and left the store without paying for them. The store manager saw the shoplifter and followed the man as he walked into the parking lot, asking him to give back the boots. The man denied having the boots, but the manager told him he saw him put them in his pants. At that point, the man displayed a firearm, told the manager to "back off," ran to a car, and drove away.

   When a circuit court found the man guilty of robbery and use of a firearm in the commission of a robbery, the man appealed the conviction. A year later, an appeals court dropped the charges, stating that the evidence was insufficient to prove a robbery because the gun was not actually used to steal the boots—only to "assist in the retention of the boots or to facilitate (the man's) escape." The appeals court authorized a new trial—this time, for larceny (shoplifting).

- A man charged for his involvement in three armed robberies of neighborhood stores was tried before a jury and found guilty of eight counts of robbery, eight counts of possessing an instrument of crime (PIC), and seven counts of conspiracy. The total sentence was 10 to 20 years for each of five robbery convictions, 10 to 20 years for two of the conspiracy convictions, and another 2.5 to 5 years for a single PIC conviction.

   The man appealed, saying he was being given what amounted to an unfair life sentence—that at age 20, he was a first-time offender who had never discharged his gun during the robberies.

   From the court decision: "(The man) apologized to the court and to his family for being in this predicament, but he neither expressed sympathy for the victims nor admitted his guilt: 'I am not gonna say that I did it or did not do that, but certain things happened around people you can't do nothing about.'

   "The *modus operandi* of (the man) and his co-conspirators was to overwhelm a store with an extreme show of force. Acting in groups of four or five, all members pointed revolvers and shotguns at their victims and threatened to kill them during the robberies. For the most part, [the man] would place his .44 magnum handgun directly to the side of a victim's head when demanding money. The evidence was that, on two occasions, [the man] did this in the presence of his victim's child . . . Despite five positive identifications from victims and a jury verdict of guilt, [the man] continued to deny his involvement during the presentencing hearings."

   The court upheld the sentences.

Sources: Excerpts of publicly documented court cases on FindLaw.com, a division of Thomson/West, Eagan, Minnesota, and Rominger Legal, a division of Rominger, Inc., Carlisle, Pennsylvania.

Make sure every witness who receives a subpoena gets to the arraignments, hearings, and/or trial for which he or she has been subpoenaed, and understands that all testimony given in court must be accurate, impartial, nonprejudicial, and truthful. Cases have been lost, and civil suits for defamation filed, because complainants and witnesses failed to appear in court—or presented inaccurate, biased, and/or untruthful testimony.

If there are unusual or extenuating circumstances in the case, be sure to explain them to the prosecuting attorney or related investigators as soon as possible.

Exercise extreme caution in discussing armed robberies, especially before they are brought to trial. As with shoplifting incidents, cases can be blown by careless discussion of robbery incidents. They should not be discussed with anyone except involved store personnel, the police, and the prosecuting attorney, until after a verdict has been reached or a plea has been made and accepted by the defendant.

ARMED ROBBERY PREVENTION CHECKLIST

Make and follow specific cash management procedures to minimize the amount of loss caused by an armed robbery.

- ❏ Make frequent withdrawals of funds from the cash registers; use drop boxes or slot safes.
- ❏ Install and use a secondary, hidden safe.
- ❏ Make multiple bank deposits throughout the day, or hire an armored car service to pick up cash and checks.
- ❏ Take special safety precautions (from Chapter 1) when opening and closing the store; avoid complacency, and vary your common routines.
- ❏ Train all employees to spot suspicious behavior.
- ❏ Train all employees about what to do (and not to do) in the event of an armed robbery.
- ❏ Incorporate these policies and procedures into the store's written operations manual.

CHAPTER SUMMARY

This chapter examined ways in which both physical danger and monetary loss can be reduced in the event of an armed robbery.

- ■ **Key safety and security issues** include the sage advice: Never argue with a gun. Accept the fact you have no control over someone brandishing a firearm and demanding money. The chapter mentioned the reasons robbers (both professional and amateur) are often unstable, nervous, and easily provoked.

■ **Pre-robbery actions** should focus on accomplishing routine tasks in ways that are *not* routine. This keeps you more alert day to day and keeps robbers from being able to study your patterns and hit the store when it is most vulnerable. A huge part of any retailer's loss prevention program is the implementation of logical cash management policies: Make frequent cash "pulls" from registers, and install drop boxes or slot safes to limit everyone's access to cash—employees as well as would-be robbers.

■ **During an actual robbery** is no time for heroism. It is best to cooperate with robbers, without volunteering "extra" cash or information. Your most important job in these harrowing moments is to keep employees and customers safe while you remain extremely attentive to any shred of evidence that might eventually help law enforcement catch the criminal(s). The chapter also detailed the major steps to take immediately following an armed robbery incident. It is exceedingly important that things you (and other witnesses) noticed be written down separately. Although emotions are high, it is smarter to keep chatter to a minimum and commit the details to paper, with each person doing so separately, to assist the police in their investigation.

■ Finally, understand that **a store owner or manager may be required to appear in court** multiple times in connection with a robbery, at arraignments and hearings as well as the trial. Be sure every witness who gets a subpoena takes it seriously and doesn't gossip about it with others, or the case may be jeopardized.

With the right policies and thorough employee training, you *can* control the financial losses and reduce the danger of personal injury to you and your retail employees.

DISCUSSION QUESTIONS

1. What might the toy store mentioned in the first paragraph of this chapter have done in advance of the fatal robbery to avoid it?
2. What is the most important thing to remember about the "average" armed robber?
3. Are there any circumstances under which you should confront or challenge an armed robber? If so, describe them.
4. Why should the store manager or owner take the lead in communicating with an armed robber?
5. Of the list of important things to keep in mind while a robbery is occurring, which do you think would be the most difficult *for you*—and why?

6. List and briefly describe three ways to reduce the physical risks and/or financial losses associated with armed robberies.

7. Look online for a news story (anywhere in the world) about a recent armed robbery of a retail establishment. Find out as much as you can about it, and write a report about what happened and, in your opinion, what the store did right—and wrong. What security suggestions would you have in this case?

8. How would you handle a situation in which you, as a store manager, believe a suspect should be charged in a foiled robbery, but the local prosecuting attorney doesn't seem all that interested in pursuing the case?

ENDNOTE

1. "Toys 'R Us Robbery Ends with Suspect Killed," Associated Press, as reported on SecurityInfoWatch.com, Cygnus Business Media, Fort Atkinson, Wisconsin, May 19, 2005.

FRAUD

Except for relatively small convenience purchases, most retail transactions today are carried out using checks and credit or debit cards—which means any of these may be used to take advantage of merchants who are not careful. This chapter addresses the ways retail businesses can minimize their losses due to fraud—check, credit card, online, and other types—that cost billions of dollars per year. Check fraud alone is a $10 billion annual "hit" for businesses, with more than 500 million forged checks annually; credit card fraud costs retailers another $2.6 billion.[1]

The subject areas in this chapter include:

- Check fraud
- Credit card fraud
- Counterfeit currency
- Fast-change and con artists
- Exchange and refund fraud
- Online fraud

Your store can be part of the solution by learning the ways various types of fraud are engineered and perpetrated, and how you can most effectively reduce their impact. It's better than being part of what is, according to the National Check Fraud Center, the fastest-growing problem in the nation's financial system.

CHECK FRAUD

There has been a tremendous increase in payments by card, but checks still play a significant role in the retail business environment. Despite persistent attempts to get people to pay their bills online, about 69 billion paper checks are still processed annually.[2] Merchants who choose not to accept checks get their share of customer complaints. Indeed, for a number of reasons, many retailers today probably could not survive if they didn't accept checks.

Checks have some good points. They encourage sales and minimize the store's vulnerability to theft and robbery by reducing the amount of cash on hand. Unfortunately, they have one major weakness. Just because you have a check in hand does not mean you have the money it represents. A third party is involved—the bank on which the check was written. Unless the bank accepts the check as a valid, negotiable instrument—that is, the check "clears" the bank—the person (or merchant) to whom the check is written winds up with nothing. To make matters worse, you suffer a double whammy: (1) you've lost your profit on the sale, and (2) you've lost the merchandise that was carried away by the bad-check passer. No wonder there are so many signs that say "In God We Trust—All Others Pay Cash!" posted on the walls of small businesses across the country.

More than 730 million checks bounce every year.[3] As a merchant, trying to determine whether a check is good or bad is like trying to pick out the shoplifters from the honest, legitimate customers who enter your store. Like shoplifting, you will not be able to completely eliminate the problem, but there are certain things you can look for and actions you can take to minimize your losses.

Types of Checks

A wide variety of checks have evolved to service the financial and commercial communities, but only a few of them are regularly encountered in the retail environment. These are as follows:

- **Personal checks** written and signed by the individuals presenting them and drawn against deposits in their own bank accounts.
- **Payroll checks** issued by an employer to a specifically named employee.
- **Government checks** issued by various federal, state, or local government agencies for a wide variety of entitlement, tax refund, pension, or salary purposes.
- **Two-party checks** written by one party (the individual against whose bank account the check is drawn) and made payable to a second party who, in turn, endorses it to a third party. The third party presents it for cash.
- **Travelers' checks** sold in preprinted denominations by large firms (banks and credit card companies) to tourists, business travelers, and others who don't want to carry large amounts of cash. Traveler's checks are first signed by the user at the time of purchase, then countersigned (by the same user) when it's presented for payment.
- **Certified checks** issued by banks. They bear on their face the bank's guarantee of the availability of the funds and the validity of the signature.
- **Money orders.** Although technically not checks, money orders are often used in the same kinds of transactions. Because they are issued for specific amounts, they are rarely used to make retail purchases. Some merchants will accept them, however, especially when presented to cover previously written bad checks or to make payments on open accounts.

Bad Checks Defined

A "bad check" is one that has been refused by a bank for payment. There are typically two types of bad checks: (1) those presented by persons who make no attempt to hide their identity and (2) those presented by persons who do not give their correct name. The first type of bad check is generally returned by the bank with the notation "Nonsufficient Funds" (NSF) or "Account Closed" (AC), which usually means the customer has overdrawn the account, inadvertently or otherwise. These checks can often be redeposited after the customer or the bank is contacted and it is verified that sufficient funds have been made available. The second type, presented by persons who attempt to hide their true identities, are usually returned by banks with the notations "Forged," "Stolen," or "No Account." These are the checks most likely to result in significant losses to the retailer.

FIGURE 6-1 Guidelines for accepting or rejecting checks.

- Allow only trained managers or supervisors to approve checks presented to the store.
- Accept personal checks for the amount of purchase only. Travelers' checks cannot be held to this rule, but be cautious about accepting large-denomination travelers' checks for small purchases.
- Only accept checks drawn on local banks, or with customers' local addresses printed on them.
- Examine carefully each check presented. *Insist that it be written and signed in your presence.* Pay particular attention to the following:
  - **Legibility.** Do not accept checks that are not written legibly. They should be written and signed in ink and should not have any written-over amounts or erasures.
  - **The date.** Do not accept checks that are undated, postdated, or more than 30 days old.
  - **The amount.** Make sure the check is written for the amount of the purchase and that the numerical and written amounts agree. Set a limit on the amount of a purchase made by check.
  - **The bank location.** Make certain the check reflects the name, branch, city, and state location of the bank on which it is drawn.
  - **The presenter's identification.** The check should have imprinted on it the name and address of the presenter.
- With the check in hand, require at least two pieces of documentation to confirm the customer's identity. Keep in mind, though, that if the check is stolen the identification presented may be stolen too. **Ask for identification that bears a laminated photograph or physical description and the signature of the bearer.** Some forms of identification are much better than others. For example:
  - Do not accept as identification easily obtained or easy-to-forge documents such as social security cards, business cards, library cards, and insurance cards.
  - Accept (after close examination and comparison) cards that bear laminated photographs, physical descriptions, and/or signatures: driver's licenses; government, military, and employer identification cards; major credit cards and local-store-issued cards that carry both an account number and a signature.
- Carefully compare signatures on check and corresponding IDs. Be especially wary if the individual seems ill at ease, tries to distract you, or seems to be slow and unusually meticulous in signing his or her name.
- If you become suspicious of fraud, try to stall the suspect and call the police immediately. If you are unsuccessful in detaining the suspect until the police arrive, get a good description of the person, any accomplices involved, and (if possible) a description of any vehicle used and the direction of departure.
- If you approve the transaction by check, do one more thing to prevent another type of check-related loss. Before handing the receipt to the customer for his or her merchandise, write on the back "Paid by Check," and date and initial it. Some individuals knowingly write bad checks and come back to the store before the check has had time to clear the bank, to ask for a cash refund. When successful, they wind up with your money. This safeguard must be emphasized to all store employees who accept checks and/or handle refunds.

Check Acceptance Guidelines

The only effective way to minimize bad-check losses is to develop and implement precautionary check acceptance guidelines, such as those listed in Figure 6-1. Post these guidelines in the back of the store or in the employee lounge, and be sure all your salespeople and cashiers review them regularly and follow them without exception.

If you are concerned about accepting a check for a big-ticket item, you may be able to obtain a verification of the account and the availability of funds by contacting the issuing bank. Some banks, however, will only perform this service for depositors.

If your check trade is sufficiently large and your losses have become significant, you would be well advised to sign up with one of the many commercial **check verification services** now available to retailers. These high-technology systems, developed initially to stem credit card fraud, have expanded to include check fraud as well. With massive data banks, these electronic systems make verifications by comparing account numbers, cross-checking addresses, and accessing national lists of stolen checks and bad-check passers. Before contracting with such a firm, however, make sure it operates in compliance with the Fair Credit Reporting Act.

You may also want to consider granting check-cashing cards to your regular customers, based on an application they agree to fill out that is checked by an appropriate credit agency. At the very least, maintain a list of bad-check passers who have victimized you in the past. The list can be expanded through cooperative exchanges of data with other store owners or your local merchants' associations.

COLLECTION AND PROSECUTION

When a merchant is notified by the bank that a deposited check is "bad," the course of action, although limited, is quite clearly defined. It will depend to a great degree, at least initially, on the stated reason for nonacceptance and the type of check involved. If, for example, the check in question is a personal check returned for "Nonsufficient Funds," your focus will be directed toward "making it good"—that is, collecting the money. On the other hand, if it is returned as "No Account," "Closed Account," or "Forgery," there's probably only one thing you can do: seek criminal prosecution.

Collections

Unless your business is located in a high-crime area (in which case you probably won't accept many checks anyway), or your customer base is highly transient because the store is located in a major tourist area or along an interstate highway, most of your bad checks will be caused by nonsufficient funds. With some effort on your part, most of these checks are collectible. The same holds true, but to a lesser extent, for checks returned because of closed or nonexistent accounts. Do not procrastinate, however. Prompt action on your part is required, and this is no time to worry about alienating or embarrassing a customer.

When a check is returned because of nonsufficient funds, contact the customer, notify the person of the stated reason for the return, and inform him or her that unless the check is redeemed in person immediately, you will redeposit it. Be sure to mention that, if the check is returned a second time, you will have no alternative but to take other legal action. *Do not accept another personal check as payment!* People who offer this kind of restitution are usually just trying to buy more time.

If this course of action proves unsuccessful, or you are unable to contact the customer, you will have to initiate a collection action. First, send the customer a notice of the returned check via registered mail, return receipt requested. This is the so-called "5-day letter" (or "10-day letter," depending on your local jurisdiction) that must be sent before a merchant can initiate criminal prosecution. The notice should be accompanied by a copy of the check and a summary of your state's bad-check laws.

Figure 6-2 is a sample five-day letter. Before initiating it, however, a retailer should contact the store's attorney, the local police department check fraud unit, or your prosecuting attorney's office for help with proper formatting and phraseology for your area.

As a final collection method, you might ask your servicing bank to put the check on "**collection status**." Your bank will then return the check to the issuer's bank, and when sufficient funds are deposited in the issuer's account (if one exists), the check will receive priority payment.

If any of these actions are unsuccessful—the registered notice brings no response, and follow-up telephone calls prove useless—as a last resort, you may turn the matter over to a collection agency. Be prepared, however, to pay the agency a significant percentage of any funds collected. Beyond those actions, your only recourse is to seek criminal prosecution.

Prosecution

After all collection efforts have failed, take your registered-letter receipt (or the letter itself, if it was returned to you as undeliverable) and the check in question to the check fraud unit of your local police department to initiate prosecution proceedings.

Take good care of the check; it is your evidence. Place it in a sealed envelope,

FIGURE 6-2 Sample of "five-day letter" form for collecting on bad checks.

Date: _____

To: _____

_____

_____

We hereby give you notice that Check # _____, dated the _____ day of _____ 20_____, drawn by you on the _____ bank of _____ (State), and payable to the order of _____, in the amount of _____ dollars, has been dishonored by nonpayment.

Unless the amount due thereon, together with interest and protest fees (if any), is paid to the holder within 5 days after receipt of this notice, such legal action as may be necessary will be taken.

_____   _____
Company Name   Name of Official

_____   _____
Mailing Address   Title

and handle it as little as possible. Make every effort to identify the writer of the check and connect him or her with the receiving of specific merchandise from your store. A good practice is to have the person who approves the check initial it, date it, and note on it a brief description of the item purchased. This can be an asset when you are preparing for or giving courtroom testimony.

If the police decide to pursue the prosecution, you will be asked to complete certain forms that must be approved by the check issuer's bank. A warrant for the issuer's arrest will then be issued. *Once a warrant has been issued, do not—under any circumstances—allow the issuer of the check to "make it good."* Such a decision can only be made by the prosecuting attorney or the judge hearing the case.

If the police determine that the amount of the check does not justify the expenditure of their resources, your only recourse will be to have your attorney file a civil complaint. A subpoena will then be issued and a court date set.

BEWARE OF CHECK WASHING

One of the fastest-growing types of check fraud is **check washing**. The perpetrators are most often mail thieves who open bills, erase the ink on a check with chemicals found in common household products, and rewrite the newly "blank" checks to themselves—substantially increasing the amounts payable. They don't tamper with the signature on the check, so they are usually not caught until the check clears and the account holder notices the discrepancy or starts bouncing checks and can't figure out why his or her account is suddenly short of funds. The forgers also create false identification documents to enable them to cash the checks quickly.

In some parts of the United States, police and U.S. postal inspectors have formed task forces to try to curb check washing. In 1998, a gang in South Florida pilfered the mail of 177 people, changed the check amounts, assumed fake names, and cashed them at 27 banks and credit unions for a total of $650,000 before being busted. Nationally, check washing nets criminals $815 million a year.

Police say you can avoid becoming a victim by depositing mail directly at a U.S. Post Office or giving it to your mail carrier personally, and locking your own mailbox.

Source: National Check Fraud Center, Charleston, South Carolina.

CREDIT CARD FRAUD

The use of credit cards, in all their various forms and as issued by banks, department stores, oil companies, and other private organizations, is central to the successful operation of today's retail establishment. With over 1 billion cards in use, the potential for increased sales is enormous. Unfortunately, so is the potential for fraud.

Unlike check fraud, however, many retailers don't see credit card fraud as a major problem. This is primarily because, if the credit transaction is handled properly, any subsequent financial loss will be absorbed by the card issuing firm, not the retailer—a significant difference from the total loss retailers often face when stuck with a bad check.

This is a shortsighted view, however, because the billions of dollars lost by credit card issuers due to fraud is recouped from retailers and consumers alike in the form of higher annual fees and interest rates.

Types of Credit Card Fraud

There are a few major criminal credit card laundering operations, but the average retailer is most likely to be confronted by two types of credit card fraud: (1) point-of-sale fraud using stolen or counterfeit cards and (2) remote fraud via telephone or Internet orders. In the latter case, the criminal uses a stolen or fake card, or gets real credit card numbers from a discarded receipt or other documentation, and/or through online theft—often using the practice known as **phishing**, in which thieves pose as legitimate businesses (banks, credit card companies, and so on) and send official-looking e-mail messages prompting their unsuspecting "customer" to "verify" his or her account information, which is then promptly stolen.

The use of stolen credit cards or credit card numbers, and the opportunistic misuse of lost cards, is usually the province of individual criminals, while the use of altered or counterfeit cards most often indicate organized gangs or crime rings. The latter threaten the very existence of many credit card issuing agencies, with altered cards being almost impossible to detect. For all its crime prevention benefits, technology has had at least one negative impact: The increasing sophistication of printers and computer-based graphics programs now puts the ability to manufacture or alter credit and debit cards well within the reach of individuals. The most common "remanufacturing" activities include re-embossing account numbers, altering signature panels, and counterfeiting the magnetic strips.

Industry Safeguards

Trying to keep one step ahead of criminals is a never-ending task for credit card issuers. New technology to produce tamperproof cards is constantly being tested and implemented. Among the safeguards currently in use are holograms, three-dimensional pictures imbedded into the face of the cards that are difficult to reproduce. Other safeguards include cardholder photographs, indent printing on the signature panel, and multiple card validation codes.

Most new safeguards require the merchant to use point-of-sale computer-terminal verification systems. Electronic verification systems are currently used to process more than 75 percent of all credit card transactions. The systems are very effective, but they do not relieve the retailer of all responsibility.

The payment of customer charges by credit-card-issuing agencies is neither automatic nor guaranteed. Payment will not be made if the retailer fails to process the charge sale properly, making it even more important for all employees that handle charge sales to be aware of the credit-card-processing procedures listed in Figure 6-3. Post these guidelines in the rear of the store or in the employee lounge, and be sure they are reviewed and/or updated regularly.

- Credit cards are the property of the issuing companies and may be recalled at their discretion. When one is presented to make a purchase, the salesperson should retain possession of it until the verification process has been completed and the authorization granted.

- Closely examine the credit card presented. Make sure the expiration date has not passed.

- If for some reason your store isn't equipped with card-reader verifiers (or the system is overloaded or otherwise "down"), check the card number against the card recovery bulletins and "stop lists" provided by the card issuer.

- Do not exceed established floor limits without obtaining authorization.

- Use the proper form for the charge card presented.

- Ensure that all copies of the transaction slip are legible.

- Make sure the sales slip is signed in your presence. Be especially wary if the purchaser seems ill at ease, tries to distract you, or is slow or unusually meticulous in signing his or her name.

- *Compare the customer's signature on the sales slip with the signature on the card. They must match.* This is the single most important check that can be made to detect fraudulent use of credit cards. If the charge card has not been signed, or if the signatures on the card and on the sales slip do not match, ask for additional identification that bears a photograph, physical description, and signature.

- Be suspicious of cardholders who make multiple purchases, all under the store's floor limit; or those who rush in, select merchandise rapidly, and keep the amount under the floor limit.

- If you suspect fraud, attempt to stall the suspect and call the police immediately. If you can't detain the individual for the police, get a good description of the suspect, any accomplices involved, and, if possible, any vehicle used and the direction of departure.

FIGURE 6-3 Procedures for evaluating credit cards.

COUNTERFEIT CURRENCY

The same rapid technological advances that make it possible for individuals to create counterfeit credit cards have also caused tremendous increases in currency counterfeiting worldwide, forcing currency redesign by governments and improved anticounterfeiting measures by retailers. The United

- The best way to detect a counterfeit bill is with a counterfeit currency detector pen—a cheap, simple, quick, and reliable screening device that requires minimal training.
- You can also simply compare the suspected bogus bill with a genuine note of the same denomination. This is easier to do if all cash registers are kept orderly, with all bills segregated by denomination, face up and in the same direction. In this case, look for differences, not similarities. Pay particular attention to the characteristics of the paper and to the quality of the printing.
- Genuine currency is printed on special paper imbedded with tiny red and blue fibers that are visible to the naked eye and can even be picked off the paper if first loosened. Counterfeiters attempt to duplicate these fibers by using a separate printing process. Close examination will reveal that they are surface-printed and are not the randomly dispersed and imbedded fibers found in genuine notes.
- The newest genuine currency also has a **watermark** and an internal metallic strip that can be seen when held up to a light, and that has the amount of the denomination written on it repeatedly.
- Watch out for "washed out" currency. The production of genuine currency requires not only the skills of master engravers, but the use of specially designed and very expensive printing equipment, both usually beyond the means of most counterfeiters. As a result counterfeit notes frequently look "washed out" and flat.
- Look for details. Most counterfeit currency lacks fine detail, especially in the area of the portrait. On a genuine note, the lines in the portrait background form distinct squares; on the counterfeit, many of these squares may be filled in.
- Examine the Treasury seal and the Federal Reserve seal for comparative purposes. On a genuine note, the sawtooth points surrounding these seals are clear and distinct; on the counterfeit, they are frequently blurred and ragged.
- Check the serial numbers. On legitimate currency, they are evenly spaced and aligned; on counterfeits, they often are not.

FIGURE 6-4 Guidelines for identifying counterfeit currency.

States in the past few years has replaced almost all of its paper currency with new bills that include several difficult-to-duplicate features.

The use of **counterfeit currency detector pens** by retailers has also become ubiquitous. These inexpensive pens are simple, quick, reliable screening devices; your cashier or other sales person makes a small mark on any U.S. bill—a mark that stays amber if the bill is good and turns dark if it isn't.

If you detect a counterfeit bill or have reason to believe someone is trying to use one in your store, take custody of both the bill and your merchandise, and call the police or the U.S. Secret Service, which is the agency with primary jurisdiction over U.S. currency counterfeiting. If the bill passer can't be detained, at least try to get a good description of the suspect, any accomplices involved, and, if possible, any vehicle used and the direction of departure. Do not surrender the bill to anyone but the police or Secret Service agents.

Without proper cash-handling procedures and detection methods for employees who man the cash wrap stations, you will miss counterfeit bills at the point of sale. If this happens, your bank generally finds the bogus bills when it goes through your cash deposits. In such cases, the bills will be confiscated and your account debited accordingly. The anticounterfeiting guidelines listed in Figure 6-4 can help reduce merchants' exposure to this type of loss.

Unlike most check and credit card fraud, those who pass counterfeit bills are often not counterfeiters. Many bogus bills are passed along by totally innocent people who have received them in change somewhere else and don't realize they are counterfeit. Thus, you must be careful in such situations that you don't risk the same legal problems incurred when you confront and/or detain "clean shoplifters." If you treat someone who is a fellow victim of counterfeiting fraud as a criminal, it could cost you much more than if you'd simply swallowed the loss represented by the bogus bill. At the time of sale, it can be a very tough call.

FAST-CHANGE AND CON ARTISTS

Fast-change artists take your money by trick and sleight-of-hand; **con artists** talk you out of it. Either way, they are vultures who prey on the naive, the inattentive, and the untrained. With their exceptionally fertile imaginations and innovative ruses, these smooth-talking hustlers are responsible for millions of dollars of losses suffered by the retail community every year.

Unfortunately, most victimized store owners don't even realize they've been fast-changed or conned; they often attribute (and blame) such register shortages on simple cashier errors. Thus, to have any hope of thwarting these slick criminals, it is imperative that everyone who handles sales transactions be knowledgeable about their basic tactics.

Fast-Change Artists

Fast-change artists are the magicians of the criminal world. With their constant stream of comments, questions, and distracting chatter, accompanied by rapid currency manipulations and exchanges, fast-change artists can literally make money disappear. They are exceptionally adept at confusing inexperienced cashiers during the change-making phase of sales transactions. Some act very friendly and sincere; others express indignation and outrage and are verbally abusive. However, they all have the same purpose in mind—to separate the store from its money through sleight-of-hand and other distractions.

A subclass of the fast-change artist is the currency switcher. Technically, currency switchers commit a form of counterfeiting: they employ the use of altered paper notes, which they usually attempt to "spend" while using some of the same chatter-and-distract tactics as the fast-change artist. For instance, these individuals may take a number of $20 bills, cut or tear one numerical value corner from each of them (they will still be negotiable) and then paste these corners on a lower-denomination bill. After some smoothing out, sanding, and color blending, these "raised" bills are then passed to busy cashiers in the hope that the alteration won't be noticed. If it is, they simply protest (often loudly and indignantly) that the bill was given to them in change at some other location. They will try to take it back and then angrily exit the store to try the ruse someplace else. Like most other forms of fast-change fraud, currency switching is easily detectable if your sales personnel pay attention—in this case, by matching the portrait and back-side art, not just the numbers on the corners.

Con Artists

The true con is an award-worthy actor who relieves people of their money by first gaining their *con*fidence (hence the term *con* artist) with convincing and often elaborate ruses. The term is used to describe some individuals who engage in various check, credit card, exchange, and refund schemes, but the persons we're concerned with here are the purists: calculating, innovative, imaginative cons of both genders, who prey on your point-of-sale operations.

An example of a con artist ploy are teams of "flashers" impersonating U.S. Secret Service agents who successfully walk away with merchants' "counterfeit" currency in an intricate and utterly convincing scheme. An entire book can be written on con artist tales and techniques, which constantly evolve; no sooner does one ploy become overused and played out than another is developed to take its place. Some tactics, however, are classics and, with different characters and ingenious adaptations, go on forever. Here are two of those classics:

- **Classic Con #1.** A teenager selects a retail store checkout lane for two reasons: it's busy and it is staffed by a young, apparently inexperienced cashier. The teen makes a small purchase, pays for it with a $20 bill, takes the change and merchandise, and exits the store.

Further back in the line (two or three people behind the teenager) is an elderly woman dressed in shabby clothing. When it is her turn at the register, the woman purchases several small items and pays for them with a $5 bill. After receiving her change, and while the cashier bags the merchandise, the woman pauses, rummages through her purse, gets a very concerned look on her face, and (in a quavering voice) says to the cashier, "I'm afraid you made a mistake; I gave you a $20 bill and this is only change for a five." The clerk replies, "I don't think so, ma'am; I'm quite sure you only gave me a five."

At this point, the con kicks in. The woman starts to sob and then, in a loud, emotional voice, begins to relate a sympathy-engendering story about being in line at the welfare office earlier in the day and running into an old friend there. Wanting to jot down the new telephone number of the friend but not having any other paper handy, she wrote the number on the *only* $20 bill she had in her possession. Setting the hook, the woman states, "That *has* to be the $20 bill I gave you. You just look in your register. The number written on it is 415-6785. You just look in your twenties. I'm sure you'll find it."

The cashier, by now taken in by the woman's situation and sincerity, begins to believe that perhaps she did, in fact, make a mistake. She opens the register and, lo and behold, there's the $20 bill with the telephone number on it, just as the woman predicted. By this time, people are watching and the line is backing up. The cashier, now perhaps completely flustered, takes out the $20 bill, apologizes profusely to the woman, and either hands her the bill or gives her $15 to supplement the change from the $5 bill. The old woman, dabbing at her eyes, puts the profit from the con in her purse and exits the store.

She then goes out into the parking lot, joins the teenager (actually her grandson), and together they drive off to find their next victim. Her grandson-accomplice had dropped off the marked bill and she got back at least $15 in profit—or maybe even *your* twenty dollars.

■ **Classic Con #2.** On a busy Saturday afternoon in your hardware store, you are honored by a visit from "The Paint Man." Wearing suitably paint-spattered work clothes, he comes in, browses around for a bit, and—when he determines that he is not being observed—removes two gallons of paint from a display. He then approaches your service counter and states, "Say, I really overestimated when I bought this paint here last week. I have a couple of gallons left over. Can you give me a refund? I looked for my receipt but I couldn't find it. It must have gotten thrown out when I was cleaning up."

When you inform him that store policy prohibits a refund without a sales receipt, he then asks instead if he can exchange "his" two gallons for a couple of gallons in another color, because his wife now wants him to paint the bedrooms. That usually works, but if it doesn't, he plays his ace:

"Well, I guess I can always use these for touch-up and maybe for doing some other rooms. Take care, I'll see you."

He then strolls out of the store with two gallons of your paint. And you can rest assured that he didn't take the economy brand; he picked the premium, $30-a-gallon, one-coat-covers, top-of-the-line product. Congratulations! You are now eligible for entry into the not-so-exclusive Paint Man Victim's Club. This scam is one of the oldest refund fraud games around. It has countless variations and has been adapted to work with a variety of products.

Preventive Measures

Minimizing losses caused by fast-change and con artists is relatively simple. It is a never-ending process of making all employees aware of the problem, stressing constant vigilance, and implementing some basic cash-handling safeguards. Make sure your employees follow the procedures in Figure 6-5.

Instruct all cash-handling personnel to check their gullibility at the door when reporting for work. They must be trained and constantly vigilant about the existence of con artists. They should question the stories told to them by "customers" who attempt to separate them from their (your) money.

- Closely examine all money received from customers, to see that it has not been altered or does not appear to be counterfeit.

- Never place the customer's money into the register drawer immediately upon receipt. Instead, place it in an open spot and leave it there until the proper change has been counted out and given to the customer, and the sale is concluded.

- Count the change for transactions twice, once to yourself and again as you give it to the customer. (*Important note:* Please teach your employees *how to make change correctly*—by counting it back to the customer, starting with the amount of the sale and working "backward" to the amount originally handed to the cashier. This reinforces the fact that, indeed, the cashier *knows* how much money was handed to him or her.)

- Of prime importance, close the register drawer immediately and call for the manager or a supervisor if any customer questions the amount of change given or attempts to confuse you in any way. The manager or supervisor can then, in the presence of the customer, check or otherwise take a reading of the register and resolve the problem.

FIGURE 6-5 Guidelines for thwarting con artists.

The "Hostage" Con

Most cons are relatively painless, except for the ache in your wallet, but the **hostage con** is an incredibly stressful and traumatic experience. Like most cons, it has various adaptations but usually works something like this: While working in your store one evening, you answer a telephone call and hear a gruff voice delivering some terrifying news: "I know you are Mr. Wilson of 2705 Cloverdale Lane. We are holding your wife and daughter hostage. Do as you are told and no one will get hurt. If you don't, you will never see them again. Your every move is being observed. Place five thousand dollars, in small bills, in a small box outside the rear door of the store. Do it within five minutes and don't call the police, and everything will be OK. Once we have the money, your wife and daughter will be released. You can talk to them in about 30 minutes. Don't call before then. Move!"

If you are like most store owners, you gather the money, place it outside as you were told, and pray that no harm comes to your family. Thirty minutes later, you call home and discover your wife and daughter have spent the evening working on costumes for the school play. At first, they are surprised that you're so upset—they're fine! By the time the police are called, the money is long gone. Too bad; that would have been an excellent time to have activated a silent holdup alarm.

At this point, you can do little besides alert fellow business owners, merchants' organizations, and local law enforcement in an attempt to prevent others from being similarly victimized.

EXCHANGE AND REFUND FRAUD

In the United States, lenient retail refund and exchange policies have been the vogue since the 1970s as a way to promote customer satisfaction and store loyalty. While it's true that every purchase made does not result in 100 percent customer satisfaction, merchandise returns now represent from 7 to 15 percent of a retailer's sales. And, according to the 2003 National Security Survey, about 9 percent of returns are fraudulent, costing the retail industry about $16 billion annually.[4]

Many stores have such lax refund and exchange policies that they are inadvertently putting themselves at the mercy of thieves who specialize in taking advantage of such merchants. Some of the more common schemes include the following:

- **Trash bin searches.** Opportunists search trash bins or pick up discarded sales receipts near the front of the store or around cash registers, and then select items in the store with equivalent prices and turn them in for refunds.

- **Stolen goods returns.** Shoplifters brazenly bring back stolen merchandise for cash refunds.
- **Comparison shopper returns.** Eagle-eyed shoppers purchase an item at a discounted price and then return it—to a store that sells the same item but at a higher price.
- **Salvage buyers.** These fraudsters obtain damaged goods at greatly reduced prices and then attempt to either exchange or return them at another store for full price.
- **Bad check returns.** Bad-check passers purchase items with a check they know is no good and then, before the check has had time to clear the banking system, try to return the merchandise for a cash refund.

Taking your cues from these tactics, determine what you can do to control these types of losses. For example:

- Establish one specific location within the store for handling returns and exchanges. Some stores use their customer service counter for such transactions, which is fine, as long as it is staffed at all times with an experienced and well-trained "returns specialist."
- If possible, locate this section or counter close to the entrance to the store—the "big box" retailers, like Target and Kmart, do a good job of this.
- Place signs prohibiting customers with refunds and exchanges from entering the main body of the store unless they check in first at the refund desk or customer service counter. If your store is small enough not to warrant a dedicated counter, at least have them "check in" at the closest cash wrap (POS terminal). Such a practice will greatly stem your losses from ploys like the "Paint Man" scam outlined earlier, and from refund scam artists who pick up discarded receipts, take equivalent-value merchandise off the shelves, and then ask for refunds.
- If at all possible, and if you can do it without alienating your regular customers, institute a stringent policy of no exchanges or returns without a valid receipt.
- Insist that merchandise returned be in salable condition unless it contains defects resulting from poor product quality or a manufacturing defect. To preclude being stung by salvage buyers, do not take back any damaged merchandise unless it is accompanied by a valid receipt from your store.
- Establish specified time limits for the return of merchandise. This prevents being victimized by persons who purchase bulk quantities of out-of-date or clearance merchandise and then try to return them for credit or refund at the full price.
- Use preprinted forms for returns that include the full name, address, and telephone number of the customer making the return. Record the identity of the item and its price, and have the customer sign the form. (See Figure 6-6 for an example.)

FIGURE 6-6 Sample form for accepting returned or exchanged merchandise.

RETURN/EXCHANGE FORM

Description of Item: _____

Date Purchased: _____ Receipt: Yes _____ No _____

Merchandise: Cost _____ Tax _____ Total _____

Reason for Return/Exchange: _____

_____

TO BE COMPLETED BY CUSTOMER ONLY

Name: _____

Address: _____

City: _____ State: _____ Zip: _____

Telephone: _____

Customer Signature: _____

Signature of Refund Clerk: _____

Signature of Supervisor: _____

Attach Customer's Receipt

- Post all the store's return and exchange policies at appropriate locations within the store, and be sure your employees are familiar with them.

One additional scheme relating to refunds must be mentioned. It relates to losses caused by "insiders"—your own employees. We'll cover employee and vendor fraud more thoroughly in Chapter 8, but the number of employees who have been caught engaging in dishonest refund schemes is amazing. Then again, maybe it isn't so amazing. All a dishonest refund clerk has to do is pick up a receipt, if one is even required, fill out a form using any name listed in the local telephone book, put it and the receipt in the register, and pocket the cash equivalent.

To prevent such blatant theft, store owners must exercise careful control over the entire refund-and-exchange operation. Determine the average volume of refunds for certain time periods, so that any increase from the norm will be immediately noted. Maintain a written log. If you notice an unusual pattern, try to narrow the time period down to a specific employee on duty at the time and increase your vigilance. Check for the merchandise that was ostensibly returned.

The best way to double-check for this type of fraud is to take a number of the return forms, which show the names, addresses, and telephone numbers of the customers who supposedly made the returns, and call them or write to them. You can, in all sincerity, couch your conversation or letter to state that you are contacting them to get customer satisfaction feedback. Be aware that some recipients may be partners of your dishonest employee, but sooner or later, if an employee is engaged in a refund scheme, you will find someone who says he or she never returned an item to your store. Bingo! You just caught a thief.

Be sure that when you hire employees, you mention that you routinely contact "returns customers" for the purpose of seeking customer satisfaction feedback. Knowing that you do, in fact, randomly check merchandise returns will effectively deter most such fraud by your employees. As a side benefit, your customers will appreciate the personal attention!

ONLINE FRAUD

Most retail stores now have Internet Web sites that can accommodate online sales, almost all of which involve the use of credit cards—and, of course, all the accompanying fraud problems. According to the CyberSource Corporation's *eCommerce Fraud Survey*, there was $2.6 billion in online fraud in 2004, an increase from $1.9 billion in 2003.[5]

One reason for the increase is certainly that more and more people are becoming comfortable with shopping online. For a retail merchant, there are inherent risks in accepting credit card orders no matter where they are placed, but the Internet allows criminals to conduct their "business" with relative anonymity. Depending on the sophistication of the crooks, they can use underground programs that employ algorithms to generate mathematically valid but fictitious credit card numbers, and newsgroups and Web sites that routinely publish stolen credit card information. The trends are worrisome.

Fortunately, there are a number of ways you can reduce your exposure to online fraud, and most of them work pretty well; the $2.6 billion loss is large, but it represented only 1.8 percent of total online sales for the year. If you accept online orders, you should implement as many of these online loss prevention methods as possible, which will require hiring an experienced Webmaster to set up the most secure site possible for your business.

Keep in mind that in online fraud, the store owner typically incurs the greatest loss. That's because most credit card issuers limit legitimate cardholder liability to $50 to $100, then refuse to honor the billing from your store—and may even add a "handling fee" of some kind as well. The net result: you lose a lot, the legitimate cardholder loses a little—and the bank actually makes money on the deal. This is an infuriating reality to many merchants, and you will find a proliferation of opinions and advice online about this issue.

There are two primary ways to combat online fraud. One is to make a call to the actual cardholder or confirm the order by fax; the second is to use an automated method that is run and monitored by software. The method you choose depends on your online sales volume, your computer literacy, and/or your percentage of high-value transactions. Many merchants use combinations of both.

Telephoning the cardholder means, of course, including a "required" field in your store's online order form for the cardholder's phone number—which should be the same phone number associated with the credit card account. Before fulfilling the order, call the cardholder for order verification. This is a good practice for high-value orders even when you don't normally do this kind of checking.

Confirming the order via fax is another good way to thwart fraudulent online purchases, as well as charge-backs created when a legitimate cardholder tries to deny that he or she authorized a given purchase. You provide an online authorization form that they print out, sign, and return, along with photocopies of both sides of their credit card. (This tends to annoy legitimate customers, but they certainly can't deny its effectiveness as a fraud deterrent.)

Antifraud software and **online fraud detection services** perform several routine checks on *every online order*, then either give you a statistical likelihood that a given order is fraudulent or "flag" those that meet default or customized guidelines for possible fraud. Here are some of the areas these automated capabilities and services can detect and investigate:

- *Anonymous proxies* hide the true location and identity of the computer from which an order is made, and while some computer users have legitimate reasons for using anonymous proxies (or may have virus-infected computers), they are also a favorite of organized-crime credit card criminals. Thus, online orders from such proxies should generally be treated as high-probability-of-fraud orders and either manually checked out and confirmed or summarily declined.
- *Bank identification number checks* are a way to see if the bank issuing the credit card is located in the same country as the cardholder's residence. Legitimate card users sometimes live in a country other than that of their card's bank, but again, this is often a sign of organized foreign credit card rings that defraud American companies and individuals. Online orders from such cardholders should also be treated as medium- to high-probability-of-fraud orders and either manually checked out and confirmed or summarily declined.

- *E-mail domains* such as Hotmail, Yahoo! Mail, USA.net, Juno.com, and e-mail forwarding systems represent another "flag" area for online orders because they are anonymous and generally untraceable, even with a court order. Such Web-based domains are not normally a showstopper, because many legitimate individuals and businesses use Web-based e-mail and/or e-mail forwarding for a variety of reasons. Nevertheless, orders from Web-based e-mail addresses should usually receive additional scrutiny before fulfillment.

- *IP address locations* raise flags when software or fraud detection services match cardholder billing addresses with the physical location of the IP (Internet Provider) address and detect that the computer from which the order originates is located somewhere other than where it is claimed to be. Most fraud detection services can estimate the physical distance between the credit card billing address and the IP address—and the country, too, in most cases. One caveat here; the purchaser could be traveling or using a laptop, so while IP/billing mismatches are a cause for concern, they should be routinely verified, not summarily declined.

Overseas fraud is one of the greatest areas of concern to retailers because there is essentially no way to recover your merchandise or prosecute the perpetrator. Fraud detection services and software can reduce risks by raising flags when orders come from foreign countries using U.S.-based cards, but often there is no way to verify the legitimacy of the cardholder—or prevent them from committing "**charge-back fraud**" by declaring to their credit card company that they either never ordered the merchandise in question or never received it. Given the risks of overseas-based online fraud, you might consider refusing all foreign orders if such orders represent a small part of your total volume. The risk may not be worth the incremental increase in sales.

What about PayPal?

PayPal is a Web-based system that uses state-of-the-art antifraud methodologies and an existing financial system infrastructure to securely transfer funds between individuals and/or companies involved in online business. You may send money through PayPal for free; to receive money, you a pay a percentage of the amount received to PayPal.

Unfortunately, you can get charged back by PayPal accounts the same way you do with credit cards, and there is the added problem that PayPal accounts are sometimes stolen or just plain fraudulent. Again, PayPal orders with Web-based e-mail addresses or e-mail forwarding should be treated as "flag" accounts and given greater scrutiny before fulfillment.

FRAUD PREVENTION CHECKLIST

Check Fraud Prevention

❏ Develop and put into practice effective check acceptance guidelines (Figure 6-1).

❏ Make sure all store management personnel are knowledgeable about proper collection procedures (Figure 6-2).

❏ Train managers about the bad-check laws and prosecution procedures in your state or city.

Credit Card Fraud Prevention

❏ Make all personnel aware of the various types of credit card fraud.

❏ Develop and implement proper credit card acceptance and verification policies and procedures (Figure 6-3).

❏ Use credit card recovery bulletins and "stop lists," if verification systems are "down" or otherwise not available in your cash register terminals.

❏ Establish a floor limit for credit card charges.

❏ Emphasize to all employees that sales slips must be signed in their presence and that signatures must match those on the credit cards presented.

❏ Instruct all employees as to what they should do if they suspect fraud.

❏ Use an electronic verification and authorization system.

Counterfeit Currency Prevention

❏ Have and use counterfeit detector pens at all cash registers.

❏ Train all cash-handling personnel in how to detect counterfeit currency. (Local law enforcement personnel or your merchants' association can help with this.)

❏ Have written policies for what to do if employees suspect an attempt is being made to pass counterfeit currency.

Preventing Fraud by Con Artists

❏ Train all employees in how to identify and recognize methods used by fast-change and con artists.

❏ Train all employees regarding proper cash-handling procedures.

❏ Implement a fast-change and con artist alerting system among local retailers.

Preventing Exchange and Refund Fraud

❏ Train all employees to recognize the wide variety of exchange and refund scams.

❏ Develop a store policy and effective procedural guidelines for handling refunds and exchanges.

Continued

❏ Make sure store management utilizes and closely monitors these procedures.

❏ Post signs stating the store's refund policy.

❏ Designate one specific location within the store for handling all returns and exchanges.

❏ Staff the exchange/refund desk with an experienced employee.

❏ If possible, locate the exchange/refund desk near the entrance to the store.

❏ Make sure the sales floor and the area around the cash registers are kept clear of all discarded receipts, to preclude their being used fraudulently.

❏ Implement special procedures, including the use of specifically designed forms and the contacting of customers, to deter and detect refund fraud by store employees.

Preventing Online Fraud

❏ Learn more about how online fraud occurs and develop written procedures for your company's online transactions.

❏ Train employees to rigorously follow these procedures and report anomalies.

❏ Use a combination of automated and manual order confirmation methods to detect fraud.

❏ Avoid overseas orders if they are not a major part of your business.

CHAPTER SUMMARY

Fraud has as many faces as the criminals who try to pull it off—by check or credit card, in person, online, and so on. In this chapter we looked at the ways you can minimize fraud-related losses, including:

- **Check fraud.** The chapter described two primary types of bad checks, collection processes, and the use of verification methods and/or professional verification services. The chapter also mentions basic steps in the criminal prosecution of professional bad-check passers.

- **Credit card fraud.** There are also two types of credit card fraud, performed either in person at point of sale, or remotely, by phone or on the Internet. Again, verification systems can be used to reduce the chances that a card is fake before you accept it. It is critical to process all credit and debit card sales properly to reduce fraud risks and increase chances of reimbursement by the issuing company. Be sure the store's employees know these procedures and review them regularly.

- **Counterfeit currency.** Technological advances make it possible even for individuals to create counterfeit currency today. Despite difficult-to-duplicate features built into currency, employees must be trained to look for telltale signs of counterfeit bills and equipped with the inexpensive, easy-to-use and very reliable counterfeit currency detector pens. If you detect or suspect a counterfeit bill, take custody of it (and your merchandise) and call the police or the U.S. Secret Service. Remember that many people passing bogus bills don't know it—they are already victims of the counterfeiter, so be very careful when dealing with the individuals from whom you get counterfeit currency.

- **Fast-change and con artists.** The chapter detailed a few of the common ruses of fast-change artists and con artists. The best ways to reduce these types of losses are to stress constant vigilance and implement some basic cash-handling safeguards, which are periodically reviewed.

- **Exchange and refund fraud.** This may be limited by limiting the time allowed for customers to return or exchange merchandise, and by randomly verifying with customers that they have, in fact, returned items that show up in your accounts. Establish clear return policies, using traffic pattern tactics and random verification procedures to reduce both outside thievery and that perpetrated by employees. Don't accept returns or exchanges without a valid receipt.

- **Online fraud.** The problem of online fraud grows as more businesses choose to sell on Web sites and as customers become more comfortable ordering online. Most online fraud is credit-card-based and can be reduced with a combination of manual and automated (computerized) checking methods, detailed in this chapter.

DISCUSSION QUESTIONS

1. What are the two primary types of bad-check writers and how do you handle collecting from each type?
2. Why do you think check fraud and credit card fraud are handled so differently, in terms of the merchant's and customer's responsibilities? Do you agree or disagree with the system?
3. When you are presented with a traveler's check for payment, should the store handle it as cash, as a check, or with completely separate rules? What should the rules be for accepting it and/or verifying its authenticity?
4. Why is it important to set a "floor limit" for your store in terms of credit or debit card purchases?
5. Do some research about retail con artists, and write a short summary of a ruse not mentioned in the book to share with your classmates.
6. If you're at the cash register and suspect you have received a counterfeit bill, how do you handle the person who gave it to you?
7. What are "flashers" and how do you handle them?
8. List three ways your exchange and refund policy can be used to defraud you, and the methods you can use to prevent this kind of loss.

ENDNOTES

1. National Check Fraud Center, Charleston, South Carolina.
2. Elayne Robertson Demby, "Checks in an Electronic Age," *Credit & Collections World*, a publication of Source Media, Inc., Austin, Texas, October 2000.
3. See endnote 1.
4. National Security Survey results, "Reduce Fraud Without Losing Your Good Customers," *360 Commerce*, Austin, Texas, 2003.
5. eCommerce Fraud Survey, CyberSource Corporation, Mountain View, California, 2004.

FRAUD AND THEFT ON THE SALES FLOOR

erhaps the most frustrating types of crime for store owners to deal with are the ones perpetrated by the people who are supposed to, by all accounts, be "on *your* side"—your employees and vendors. In this chapter and the next, we address the methods through which retailers can prevent or at least reduce losses through employee theft, a category that accounts for almost half of the $31 billion U.S. companies lose each year to theft, vendor fraud, and administrative error. Perhaps it is ironic that many retailers are better organized when it comes to combating shoplifting than employee thefts, although the average loss from an employee theft is $1,341, compared to $207 for a shoplifting loss.[1]

Specific subject areas to be covered in this chapter include the following:

- How and why employees steal
- Identifying high-risk employees
- Creating controls for personnel and merchandise
- Controlling and detecting theft at the cash register
- Handling errors, voids, and other special situations
- Employee terminations and arrests

Many of the policies and procedures in this chapter are based on common sense, but as with other loss prevention/reduction techniques, they can only be effective when carefully planned, formally integrated into the store's daily management processes, and enforced routinely and consistently.

TYPES OF EMPLOYEE THEFT

This book is full of warnings and admonitions regarding employee theft. Among those mentioned were the dishonest assistant manager who reenters the store after closing to remove merchandise. Employees throw merchandise in trash bins or out windows to waiting accomplices, or perhaps stash it in ducts or vents for later retrieval. Sales personnel "**slide**" merchandise to their friends, take part in collusive acts with vendors, or engage in fraudulent refund schemes.

In addition to the methods already mentioned, here are some of the more common ways in which employees steal merchandise and embezzle funds:

- **Simple theft.** Frequently (and in our view, improperly) minimized by being referred to as "pilferage" or "toting," this is shoplifting by employees— removal from the store of merchandise concealed in pockets, purses, backpacks, and so on.
- **Collusive theft.** Merchandise is removed by two or more employees working together—for example, a sales clerk and a janitor. The term also refers to thefts caused by employees working as partners with outsiders, such as vendors and trash collectors.
- **Product substitution theft.** Employees (like shoplifters) may remove expensive merchandise by placing it in a box from a less expensive product. Collusion with outsiders is usually involved.
- **Employee purchase theft.** More merchandise is taken than was actually paid for.
- **Inventory theft**. Deliberate "short-counting" of merchandise may be used to cover up a current or previous theft. (This topic will be covered in Chapter 8.)

- **Shipping and receiving theft.** Employees, acting alone or in collusion with others, falsify carton or item counts when deliveries are first made (before the items are on the sales floor) and steal the merchandise. (This topic will be covered in Chapter 8.)
- **Embezzlement at the POS terminal.** Sales are under-recorded or not recorded at all on the register, and the equivalent amount of money is taken; or false errors and voids are claimed, and the cash equivalents are removed from the register. False refund schemes are also included in this category.
- **Accountant or bookkeeper embezzlement.** A wide variety of schemes relate to cash reports, the accountability of funds, and bank deposits. Figures are manipulated, money is taken from register receipts that have been turned in, and bank deposits are deliberately shorted. Also, receipts for payouts made to vendors are raised, and fraudulent receipts for store expense items are created. Thefts from petty cash accounts are accomplished, usually by altering existing vouchers or creating fictitious ones. (Again, this is discussed in Chapter 8.)
- **Managerial embezzlement.** The schemes are similar to those employed by dishonest accountants and bookkeepers; however, the amounts stolen are larger when senior managers are involved, and the theft frequently involves the creation of "dummy" suppliers and "ghost" employees.

Unfortunately, these are only a few examples. Employees, like shoplifters and con artists, have fertile imaginations and can dream up countless ways to separate a store from its money and merchandise. If there is *need* and *temptation*, all a dishonest employee then requires is *opportunity*—which is where loss prevention comes in. The more you narrow (or shut) the windows of opportunity for employee theft, the less likely it will be that they will steal, regardless of temptation or need.

WHY EMPLOYEES STEAL

Criminologists and sociologists conduct endless studies and have strong feelings about why some people engage in dishonest acts and others don't. Case studies of retail employee crimes tend to reflect the three factors just mentioned as significant contributors to the problem: need, temptation, and opportunity.

In most cases, the need is actual or perceived financial desperation brought on, for example, by the loss of a full-time job, emergency medical expenses, unexpected automotive repairs, or other personal misfortune. The need for more money could also be symptomatic of someone who is a gambler, an alcoholic, or a drug abuser.

Need can also be defined as desire. An example of desire as a motivating factor can be found in the young, part-time sales clerk who desires friend-ship and wants to stimulate her popularity with her schoolmates. To achieve her goal, she undercharges or does not even ring up the purchases they make in her department.

The temptation factor is more subtle and much more insidious. It relates not only to the clichéd analogy of placing the "fox in the henhouse," but also to the development of a mental attitude within the employee that culmi-nates in a perceived justification for committing the dishonest act. A prime example is the employee who steals because, rightly or wrongly, he or she feels underpaid, unappreciated, or treated unfairly.

The final factor, opportunity, does not require any further definition. If there is a need and a perceived justification, all a misguided or dishonest employee requires is the chance to steal and your merchandise or money is gone. You have very little control over the need and the temptation, but you have enormous control over the opportunity. *If you can establish sufficient internal controls, you can significantly reduce the opportunities for employees to steal.* The establishment of such controls, however, is only half the battle; you must also implement and enforce them consistently.

Identifying High-Risk Employees

To develop an effective, dedicated, and honest workforce, you must get to know your people. You must treat them fairly and equitably and be attuned to their personal problems and concerns. When employees are emotionally upset and distraught because of outside circumstances, their performance will obviously suffer, which, in turn, could have an adverse effect on your business. Be sympathetic and understanding, and help them when you can. Not only is it the humanitarian thing to do, but your concern will be repaid a hundredfold in superior job performance, enhanced employee loyalty and, most importantly, trustworthiness.

In addition, your interest will enable you to spot those individuals who are at risk—the ones whose personal affairs, lifestyles, and habits identify them as being perhaps a bit more susceptible to dishonesty. Pay particular attention to the following signals:

- Significant indebtedness
- Questionable associates
- Excessive drinking
- Gambling
- Drug abuse or addiction (illegal or prescription)
- Living beyond means (place of residence, type of vehicle driven)
- Noticeable mood swings, personality changes
- Marital or partnership problems

- Unusual or secretive work habits (first to arrive, last to leave, no vacations, etc.)
- Frequent, prolonged visits by the same customers
- Unusually friendly relationships with vendors
- General unhappiness and/or apparent dissatisfaction with job, spouse, school, life, and so on

Now let's test your instincts. A customer at a Wal-Mart store in Rochester, New Hampshire, was standing in a checkout line and noticed that for the people just ahead in line, the cashier only seemed to be scanning the bar codes of inexpensive items—not the large, electronic items they also had. The alert customer followed the people out of the store, wrote down their vehicle license number, and reported it. An investigation uncovered a theft ring that involved collusion between two cashiers and their two "customers." Knowing what you now know about the reasons for employee theft, what could this store have done to determine whether these cashiers (both females, ages 18 and 19) were at high risk for criminal behavior? How could the store have honed in on this type of collusive theft, without the aid of an observant (and honest) customer?[2]

INTERNAL CONTROL PROCEDURES

The prevention of internal losses requires a multifaceted approach, and while it is clear that certain controls must be established, a realistic balance must be maintained to prevent creating a stifling, oppressive work environment in which every employee feels suspect. An overly aggressive, heavy-handed approach will only alienate your staff members and make it very difficult for you to enlist their cooperation in all the other loss prevention issues that must also be addressed. The following internal control suggestions augment those mentioned in earlier chapters, though not all are appropriate in all work environments.

Personnel Controls

These controls relate primarily to the non-sale or non-duty movements and activities of employees.

- **Accounting for employee time.** Time is money. To control your payroll, employees should be required to use time cards or some other written method of sign-in and sign-out accountability. Monitor work habits to prevent misuse of time—people shouldn't be able to sit around on "company time" reading magazines and newspapers; computer logs can show extensive Internet use for workers with desk jobs.

■ **Entry and exit.** All employees should be required to enter and exit through a specific entryway or door. This location should be monitored, especially during shift changes and at closing, by a security guard (if one is employed) or by a supervisor.

■ **Employee parking.** If possible, do not allow employees to park their private vehicles near side or rear doors, or near the store's receiving dock.

■ **Personal belongings.** Employees should be discouraged from bringing packages into the store. These should be "checked in" in a secure area at the start of a shift and sealed or locked in a controlled setting until the employee's shift is over and he or she comes to collect them before exiting the store. Generally, it is also unwise to allow employees to keep purses, backpacks, and outer garments (raincoats and overcoats) in work areas. Make every effort to provide a separate locker room or storage closet equipped with individual lockers and located in an area that can be monitored by store management. Employees aren't fond of these measures, but they become accustomed to them. Let them know they are also being spared from their own goods being stolen from under a counter or in an unsecured area by keeping them locked up during the workday.

■ **Spot-check policies.** If there's just not room for a separate, secure area, consider having a written policy of spot-checking purses and backpacks for stolen merchandise, to which the employee must agree and sign a statement upon being hired.

■ **Employee purchases.** This topic is of special importance. When uncontrolled, purchase is one of the major avenues used by employees to steal. *Insist that all employee purchases be transacted through store management.* Designate certain time periods when workers can do their own shopping, or if purchases are made during a period of time when the employee is still on duty, the merchandise (properly bagged and sealed) should be retained by the store manager or in the office until the employee is off duty and ready to exit the store. There should never be a time when you, as a store manager or owner, do not know what an employee is carrying out of the store.

Merchandise Controls

Without the goods, there can be no business. Merchandise must be protected from damage, misuse, and theft. Previous chapters covered the threats from outsiders, so this section focuses on establishing controls to prevent employees from causing similar problems.

■ **Inventories.** Periodic inventories are an absolute must. When conducted by your own staff, they should (whenever possible) be performed on a cross-department basis. If you allow employees to inventory their own departments, you are offering them a way to cover up their own thefts. The regular use of an independent, third-party inventory firm is also recommended.

- **Stockrooms.** Access to stockrooms should be restricted, and high-value merchandise should be protected by locks and alarm systems controlled by supervisors. Merchandise should be stacked neatly, to prevent damage and make it easier to spot missing items.

- **Damaged merchandise.** Prohibit or severely limit reduced-price sale of distressed or defective merchandise to employees. This rule will deter them from deliberately damaging salable items. It will also prevent legal claims if the employee is injured in any way by a defective product purchased (albeit at a hefty discount) from your store.

- **Use of stock.** Employees should not be allowed to indiscriminately take merchandise from the sales floor or stockrooms to use for store upkeep, repair, or maintenance. The use of these materials should be first approved by a manager and then recorded and accounted for as a separate class of store expenditures.

- **Out-of-area merchandise.** Store managers should look closely at any merchandise found away from its typical area or department. There's usually a simple explanation, but when merchandise is stashed in an unusual spot or found behind the cash wrap counter, it could also mean the employee is getting ready to steal it or pass it off to a friend.

- **Concealed merchandise.** Managers should routinely check trash bins and garbage containers for perfectly good items. Why? Dishonest employees, especially janitors, frequently remove merchandise from a store for later recovery from outside receptacles and Dumpsters. Doubling-back after closing for the night and then returning to drive around behind the store to check on these Dumpsters can often be an illuminating experience. Employees can frequently be caught red-handed going through the trash to recover merchandise they have stolen.

CONTROLLING THE CASH WRAP

Effective controls at the **cash wrap** (also called a cash register or POS terminal) begin with daily opening, shift change, and closing register readings. These readings, often referred to as **Z readings**, provide a running total of all transactions that have occurred on a particular cash register. Separate readings must be taken for each drawer in a multidrawer register.

There should be no gaps in these readings. The closing reading for one day, or shift, should be the opening reading for the next. *These readings should only be taken by a store manager or owner.* Allowing sales personnel to take readings on their own registers, or to have access to the special register keys necessary to take such readings, make it infinitely easier for them to steal. One of the most common methods of embezzlement occurs when a dishonest employee, who is allowed to take his or her own register reading, closes out the register an hour or so before the actual end of the business day and uses that reading as a "total receipts" figure when turning in the register receipts. The money received from all subsequent sales that may be transacted before the store finally closes is stolen. The register detail tape is temporarily removed, or the second tape used is destroyed.

Each employee should operate from and be totally responsible for his or her own register drawer. This should make it clear who will be liable for any shortages (accidental or deliberate) that may arise. Employees who perform rotational duties, such as filling in during lunch breaks, should also be assigned their own separate drawers, with new register readings taken as appropriate. Once accountability for a cash drawer is delegated to a specific employee, store managers should not open that drawer unless the employee is present. Otherwise, it is impossible to hold that employee responsible for any shortage that may subsequently be discovered.

Operating Funds

Employees should be provided with a "**bank**," a specific amount of cash to start their shift in their particular register drawer. The first thing they should be required to do when they receive their bank for the day is, in the presence of the person who gives it to them, count it to immediately verify the amounts provided.

Managers can make a simple scruples check by occasionally engaging in a practice known as "**salting**." All you have to do is add a 10-dollar or 20-dollar bill to the fund and then sit back and wait to see whether the employee reports it.

At shift changes, the checking in and checking out of a POS terminal should be a formal, controlled process. This function should be accomplished independently, without the assistance of other employees. Employees should be required to fill out a preprinted form that lists the composition and totals of the day's receipts. The form should have blocks for recording the opening and closing readings, but these figures should not be filled in or available to register operators. Figure 7-1 is an example of a cashier's check-in and checkout form.

Managers should bear in mind that, in a busy retail environment, not all shortages are the result of theft. Most are purely accidental. Some are also humorous (though usually only in retrospect), and some are truly unbelievable. For example, did you hear about the college student who earned most of his tuition by working part-time as a cashier in a sporting goods store? Every evening when checking out, he used the cash register as an adding machine in order to save time and check his accuracy. Trying to balance out the register drove the manager crazy! Then there was the part-time checkout clerk in the

FIGURE 7-1 Sample form for checking cash register receipts.

CASHIER'S CHECK-IN/CHECKOUT FORM

Date _____

Dept _____

Reg No _____ Drawer _____

Shift _____

Cashier _____

_____

CHECK-IN

Amount of Bank $ _____

    Pennies   _____

    Nickels   _____

    Dimes   _____

    Quarters   _____

    Other Coins   _____

    Ones   _____

    Fives   _____

    Tens   _____

    Twenties   _____

    Fifties   _____

    One Hun'ds   _____

Subtotal $ _____

Over—(Short)   _____

TOTAL CHECK-IN $ _____

Signature _____

CHECKOUT

    Pennies   _____

    Nickels   _____

    Dimes   _____

    Quarters   _____

    Other Coins   _____

    Ones   _____

    Fives   _____

Continued

FIGURE 7-1 (*Continued*)

Tens	_____
Twenties	_____
Fifties	_____
One Hun'ds	_____
Checks*	_____
Credit Cards*	_____
Chg. Cards*	_____
Other*	_____
Subtotal	$_____
ADJUSTMENTS	
Less Overrings*	(_____)
Less Paid-Outs*	(_____)
Other Deducts*	(_____)
Subtotal	$_____
Less Bank	(_____)
TOTAL RECEIPTS	$_____

* Documentary Verification Required

BOOKKEEPER/MANAGER'S RECONCILIATION

Opening Reading	$_____
Closing Reading	$_____
TOTAL RECORDED	$_____
Total Adjustments	$(_____)
AMOUNT TURNED IN	$_____
Amount Over (Short)	$_____

drugstore who, every time she got a lot of change, rang it up on the register before she put it in the drawer—another nightmare for her manager.

(Speaking of change, cash register repairs are very costly. Instruct your employees *not* to break open rolls of coins on open register drawers.)

Recording Sales

This is where things really get sticky, especially when coping with sticky-fingered employees. Company policies must clearly state that *all sales are to be rung up immediately and completely, and the register drawer is to be closed after every transaction.* Purchases should not be combined; each item must be recorded separately. Sales personnel should not be allowed to make any type of adjustment or correct an error by improperly recording the price of the next item. *The customer's receipt must accurately reflect the exact price of each item purchased.* Failure to adhere to these policies allows most register thefts to occur.

Register thefts, often referred to as "knocking down" and "till tapping," are accomplished in numerous ways. For example, while operating a busy front checkout register, a cashier leaves her drawer open. As people rush through, she makes change from it, never or only occasionally recording a sale properly. The money that never actually makes it into the drawer, is later snuck aside for removal. Or a salesman deliberately under-records a sale for a customer. After the drawer is opened, he notices the "mistake," recomputes it on a handy scrap of paper, accepts the additional money, and puts it into the register—without recording it. He now has an overage in his register that, of course, he will later take. If he is clever enough and doesn't want to get caught with an overage in his drawer, he passes the overage off as change to an accomplice posing as a customer.

DETECTING SALES-RELATED THEFT

Remember, it is not just cash that disappears from cash registers. Gift certificates, food stamps, blank credit card slips, and more are all prey for enterprising thieves, so there must be a way to number and/or otherwise track each of these items. There are several methods store owners and managers can use to detect and deter thefts from the checkout staffers, including the following:

- **Alertness.** Managers must look for and be able to recognize indications of possible register manipulation. Most employees who steal keep a running tally of their "take" so they will know how much to remove when the opportunity presents itself. Look for out-of-place bills or coins in the cash drawer—pennies in the quarters slot, for example, with each penny representing a dollar to be taken. Look around the register for other items that could be used to keep count: an odd grouping of paper clips, candy, or peanuts, or markings on scraps of paper.
- **Spot checks.** To catch employees who have already pulled money out of a register (which they will subsequently make up for by under-ringing), or to catch those who have accumulated an overage in the register (which they have not yet removed), nothing can compare with the periodic spot check. Managers simply take unannounced register readings and count the receipts on hand. Besides being useful for fraud detection, this policy

FIGURE 7-2 Sample form for recording cash register discrepancies.

CASHIER'S OVER/SHORT FORM (Blue Ink=Over Red Ink=Short)															
Salesperson	Date: Two-Week Period from _____ to _____														Total Over (Short)

is an extremely effective deterrent. Use common sense when making spot checks: do not allow a set pattern to develop, such as the practice of making only one each day. Alert and devious employees will soon notice this shortcoming, then just wait until after you make your check before they start "knocking down" on their registers. Vary the numbers and the times of spot checks. Double-back and check the same employee you checked earlier. Put special emphasis on new employees.

■ **Over/short forms.** Another great asset in detecting dishonest cash wrap operators is the use of an over/short form. This is a simple, calendar-type form on which the performance of all employees over a given period of time, usually a month, is recorded in separate blocks. Overages are recorded in blue and shortages in red, to easily detect patterns and trends. These patterns, especially when erratic, often indicate improper register manipulation. They can also help pinpoint a careless or inept employee who may need additional training or who is so inept that termination is the only solution. An example of an over/short form is shown in Figure 7-2.

Errors and Voids

Register transactions are not always handled perfectly. Employees make mistakes, customers change their minds or, occasionally, discover they do not have enough money to make the intended purchase. The transaction

FIGURE 7-3 Sample form for recording cash register voids and over-rings.

VOID/OVER-RING FORM

Dept: _____   Date: _____

Register/Drawer No: _____   Transaction No: _____

Salesperson: _____

Amt Mdse Error: _____   Tax: _____   Total Error: _____

Reason: _____

_____

Signature Salesperson: _____

Signature Supervisor: _____

TO BE AUTHORIZED BY SUPERVISOR
WHILE CUSTOMER IS STILL PRESENT

(Prepare in Duplicate: 1 copy to salesperson – 1 copy to supervisor)

recorded on the register must then be corrected. Errors, voids, over-rings, or whatever else you decide to call them, must be controlled with a specific procedure. They are by far the easiest and most common ways for employees to steal from their registers.

The theft is simple—all an employee has to do is pick up a receipt discarded by a customer, mark it "Void," put it in the register drawer, and take out the equivalent amount in cash. Or, if no receipt is available, and depending on store procedures, the employee might complete some unverified form claiming an error was made, note the amount, and put the form in the register. The equivalent amount in cash, as in the previous example, can then be later removed and no one will be the wiser. At least, that's the plan.

Register errors and voids must be verified by store management at the time they occur and while the customer is still present. A formal, two-copy, preprinted form should be used. It should indicate the register location or number, the transaction number, and the amount of the error. It should be signed by both the cashier and the supervisor, with each person who signs retaining a copy. The register detail tape can also be circled and initialed by the supervisor. These forms should not be completed by sales personnel, nor should they have access to them. Figure 7-3 is an example of a void/over-ring form.

Because a register receipt must usually be available to engage in cash register embezzlements, additional attention must be focused on controlling their availability. Every effort should be made to ensure that customers receive and leave the store with their receipts. A good practice is to have sales personnel staple the receipt at the top of the bag or near the handles, or to ask, "Would you like the receipt in the bag or in your purse (or wallet)?" Today's customer, also wary of theft, may prefer to hang on to receipts for their brand-new merchandise just in case it is grabbed from them before they get it home.

Another procedure that will induce customers to take their receipts, and to pay more attention to the manner in which their transactions are recorded, is the use of specially marked register receipt tapes. Tapes are available that are randomly imprinted with company logos or designs such as stars. Signs are posted at cash registers announcing that if a logo or star appears on the customer's receipt, the customer will receive a 10 percent discount. The use of this type of system helps reduce knock-down and till-tapping activities, as well as preventing fraudulent over-rings and voids.

Refund and Exchange Controls

This subject was part of our earlier discussion of external loss prevention issues in Chapter 6, but it is an equally significant internal control problem, so we'll mention it again. Unfortunately, the biggest percentage of all refund fraud is committed by employees. When formulating an internal theft control policy, review the recommendations in Chapter 6, including the sample return/exchange form (see Figure 6-6 in Chapter 6). In addition, consider these precautions to prevent employee-related refund and exchange scams:

- **Sales to relatives.** Employees should be instructed that, in order to keep themselves free from suspicion, they should not handle transactions for members of their immediate family or for relatives.
- **Professional shopping services.** Another method of control that can be very effective is to retain the services of a professional shopping firm. Personnel from the firm, posing as regular customers, can evaluate your employees on their courtesy, appearance, job knowledge, and general efficiency. Professional shoppers are usually trained to detect employees engaged in dishonest cash register operations and other improper or illegal activities.

MISCELLANEOUS CONTROLS

Depending on the size and type of your business, there are a few more, general controls to be considered for implementation:

- Limit access to the store office and keep it locked when unattended.
- Control the use of store telephones. Allow them to be used for business and personal emergencies only.

- Establish firm policies for the use of company vehicles.
- Do not allow your employees to accept gifts, travel, lodging, or gratuities of any type from any suppliers or vendors from whom they order merchandise or whose shipments or deliveries they are responsible for checking in.

EMPLOYEE TERMINATIONS AND ARRESTS

It's an unfortunate fact of real-world retailing that sometimes terminations and arrests are the only ways some employer-employee relationships can end when theft is discovered and the perpetrator turns out to be "one of your own." Which course of action you pursue—termination or arrest—is a judgment call that only you can make. The age of the employee involved, the length of employment and position held, as well as the amount of money or value of the merchandise stolen, will be mitigating factors. Compassion and "second chances" have their place, but *all significant illegal actions by employees should result in immediate dismissal of the workers from their jobs, and their arrest.* This outcome, when shown to be with cause, will have the added impact of a significant theft deterrent to the rest of your workforce. A "zero tolerance" policy is by far the most effective.

Terminations and arrests are complex issues that must be handled with extreme care. The legal minefield to be traversed is very similar to the hazards encountered when dealing with shoplifters: You must be factually sure of what has transpired, you must have the evidence, and you must be certain you are accusing the right employee. Before pursuing any termination or arrest, you would be well advised to reread Chapter 4 on shoplifting and substitute *employee* wherever the word *shoplifter* appears. All of the same caveats apply. Pay particular attention to the discussion of confrontations, detentions, arrests, written statements, care and control of evidence, and Civil Release forms.

It is true that the store owner has some major advantages when dealing with employees rather than shoplifters. You know the identity of your suspect, they are less likely to assault you, and you have the luxury of time. In most incidents, particularly those involving embezzlements, you do not have to make an immediate decision. In fact, you can get some professional help.

Rarely is employee theft or embezzlement a one-time thing. If it happens once, it is more than likely going to happen again. If your suspicions have been aroused but you're not sure what occurred, increase your vigilance so that the next time it happens you'll be able to get the evidence you need to make an arrest. In many instances, you will be able to enlist the help of your local police or hire a private investigative firm, actions that are highly recommended.

If you actually catch an employee in the act of stealing merchandise, your reaction should be swift and sure. Recover the merchandise and decide whether you want to prosecute. If you opt to do so, call the police and let them handle it. *If you decide not to prosecute but to terminate the employee instead, do not do it without first interviewing the employee and getting a written admission of guilt.* You may use the same statement form that was developed for use with shoplifters (see Figure 4-4 in Chapter 4).

The statement itself need not be lengthy. All you really need is the full identification of the employee, the length of time employed, the position held, and a brief narration of the incident. You also need a list of the merchandise stolen and the person's written admission of guilt. Complete the document with signatures: the employee's, your own signature, and that of a witness.

If, during the interview, you get an admission that the employee has other stolen company merchandise at another location, have the employee include specific permission for you to recover it in his or her written state-ment, or have the employee sign a separate Consent to Search form (shown in Chapter 4, Figure 4-5). The employee may also admit to the theft of mer-chandise that is no longer recoverable, such as foodstuffs and other perish-ables. An itemized listing of this stolen merchandise should be made and its value determined. If, as is usually the case, the employee offers to make full restitution, the stolen merchandise list, its value, and the employee's offer of restitution should be included in the written statement.

Unless full repayment is made at the time of the interview, the employee should be asked to sign a promissory note to cover the amount of the resti-tution. An example of a promissory note is shown in Figure 7-4. This form can also be used as a means to recover monetary losses, such as thefts from a cash register, when prosecution is not pursued. After all necessary docu-ments have been signed and witnessed, and before the employee is termi-nated for a violation of company policy (stealing), have the employee sign a Civil Release form (see Chapter 4, Figure 4-6) absolving you and the store from any possible civil liability charges if any errors have been made.

As the store owner or manager, it is understandable that you just want to tell the thief to get out of your sight. You may be embarrassed, disgusted, furious—or all three. But at this point, it is extremely important to cover the legal bases. Get whatever you can in writing, dated, signed, and witnessed. It may be the last time you see this newly fired employee—and the last, best chance for you to get what amounts to a confession and any promise of repayment or recovery of property.

Of course, before a store owner ever faces the prospect of making a ter-mination or arrest, he or she should discuss these procedures with an attor-ney. It is important to fully understand the store's obligations, the owners' and managers' individual rights, and the legal requirements for pursuing such action. These should be put in writing and included as part of the store's company policies.

FIGURE 7-4 Sample of promissory note form.

PROMISSORY NOTE

Date: _____
County of: _____
State of: _____

On demand, for value received,

I, _____,

promise to pay to _____

the sum of _____ dollars

in lawful money of the United States, with interest at the rate of _____ percent per annum, interest payable monthly.

In case said interest is not paid when due, it shall be added to the principal and bear a like rate of interest until paid and the whole of said principal and interest shall forthwith become due at the option of the holder hereof without notice.

All sums shall be paid at _____

The consideration for this note is money owed by me to:

_____

and is not given in exchange for any promise, express or implied, to withhold or stifle criminal prosecution. In case suit is brought to collect this note or any portion thereof, I promise and agree to pay such additional sum as the court may adjudge reasonable for attorney's fees in said action.

_____   _____
Witness   Signature

_____   _____
Address   Address

INTERNAL LOSS PREVENTION CHECKLIST

Preventing Employee Theft

❏ Enlist the help of your local police department or merchants' association in teaching all managers about the types and exact methods of employee theft.

❏ Develop and implement personnel controls.

❏ Develop and implement merchandise controls.

❏ Train managers to routinely check trash containers for concealed merchandise.

Cash Wrap and Register Controls

❏ Make sure only store managers take daily register readings.

❏ Assign each employee a specific register drawer.

❏ Verify contents of register drawers at every shift change.

❏ Establish a formal, controlled process for register check-in and checkout.

❏ Develop written company procedures and policies about how to handle transactions, including errors, voids, and over-rings.

❏ Make cash register spot checks of all cashiers.

❏ Use over/short forms to monitor employee register performance.

❏ Require manager verification of errors and voids while the customer is still present.

❏ Develop control procedures for handling returns and exchanges.

Miscellaneous Controls

❏ Limit the use of store telephones.

❏ Establish firm policies for the use of company vehicles.

❏ Prohibit employees' acceptance of gifts, travel, lodging, and gratuities from vendors.

Employee Terminations and Arrests

❏ Develop and implement a "zero tolerance policy" for employees who are caught stealing merchandise or embezzling funds.

❏ Get a signed statement of guilt and/or promissory note before requiring the person to leave the premises.

❏ Have termination and arrest policies reviewed by an attorney to ensure legal compliance.

CHAPTER SUMMARY

In this chapter we addressed the methods through which you can prevent or at least reduce your inventory and other losses through employee theft. Chapter highlights included the following:

- **Types of employee theft.** Employees have a plethora of tried-and-true theft methods at their disposal, and this chapter explained many of them, from "slides" to product substitutions to ways that cashiers "knock down" their registers. In many cases, thefts are the joint efforts of the store's employees and outsiders, such as vendors or the worker's friends.
- **Factors contributing to employee dishonesty.** The conbination of need, temptation, and opportunity can be formidable. Your task as store owner is to create and fairly apply policies and procedures that reduce all three. Identifying high-risk employees means learning about your employees as people and recognizing potentially high-risk situations, from financial or marital problems to substance abuse issues to overly chummy relationships with vendors.
- **Prevention is about using control procedures.** Account for employee time, control employee entrance and exit, parking location, and personal possessions carried in and out. Monitor employee purchases, and realize that there is nothing sneaky about conducting spot checks or tests of your systems to see how well they are working.
- **Check-out counters (cash wraps).** The chapter mentioned ways to make each employee totally responsible for his or her own register drawer, with a formal, check-in/checkout process and rules about how to ring up all types of sales and deal with all types of anomalies—returns, voids, exchanges, and so on.
- **Employee terminations and arrests.** Proceed with caution and use the same policies and procedures described in Chapter 4's discussion about shoplifting to minimize the store's liability and maximize chances of a successful termination and/or prosecution if it becomes necessary.

DISCUSSION QUESTIONS

1. List four common types of employee theft and one policy *not* mentioned in this chapter that you think would be a good addition to a retail store's employee handbook.
2. What three elements must be present in order for an employee to steal from an employer?
3. Would you classify retail theft-prevention activities as a loss prevention function or as a cost management function? What might the difference(s) be in these two management approaches?

4. How can managers or store owners identify high-risk employees without making everyone feel they are being watched and/or mistrusted?
5. Why is it unwise to allow retail employees to keep coats, purses, and backpacks with them on the job? How would you counter an employee's argument that people *need* those items and *are* allowed to keep those items handy in other jobs?
6. How would you set up a spot-check policy, and what items would you include? What would the penalties be for "found" merchandise? For refusing to allow a spot check?
7. Many of the hints in this chapter involve doing things with the authorization of a store manager, but what if the manager is the one "on the take?" How should managers' purchases and personal belongings be "policed," and who should do it?
8. Draft a short, written policy for accepting gifts from vendors and sales representatives. Are there some instances—weddings, new babies, promotions—in which a token of congratulations would be acceptable? Spell these out in your policy.

ENDNOTES

1. National Retail Security Survey, University of Florida, Gainesville, Florida, 2002.
2. "Customer Helps Break Wal-Mart Scam," Associated Press, on www.Security-InfoWatch.com, Cygnus Business Media, Fort Atkinson, Wisconsin, June 9, 2005.

FRAUD OFF THE SALES FLOOR

T hus far we have focused on preventing thefts and fraud by sales employees and cashiers, but anywhere in the supply chain, thieves can strike hard and seriously damage retail businesses. In fact, warehouse and delivery people—whether they are your own employees or working for your suppliers— have the added advantage of working "outside" the store, with the means to easily stash stolen goods and transport them to other locations. The other key work groups to be closely monitored are the store's back-office monetary functions: accounting and bookkeeping, where theft is as easy as creating a fictitious customer or a dummy invoice.

This chapter focuses on "back-of-store" functions and loss prevention policies. Specific control areas to be covered in this chapter include:

- Preventing vendor fraud
- Developing warehouse controls
- Creating secure receiving systems
- Antitheft precautions during shipping and transport
- Legal action against vendors
- Controls for accountants and bookkeepers

Loss prevention experts are unclear about exactly how much fraud is committed by warehouse workers, delivery drivers, and the employees responsible for billing and accepting payments. The University of Florida's annual Retail Security Survey cites 5 percent of retail store losses as attributable to "vendor theft," and another 15 percent as "administrative (clerical) error," but it is widely believed that these figures are low because such crimes are either unreported or undiscovered.[1]

FRAUD BY DISHONEST VENDORS

Depending on your type of store, some of its losses may be attributable to dishonest vendors—delivery drivers, route personnel, and manufacturers' representatives. Sadly, this is especially true if the same individual services your store over a long period of time and develops a friendly, trusting association. Store employees become less vigilant, which affords the dishonest vendor numerous opportunities to engage in "short" deliveries and outright theft. Another possibility is the development of a close relationship between a vendor and an employee that results in collusion—a partnership, forged specifically to commit illegal acts. Alertness on your part, plus adherence to a few simple guidelines, can greatly reduce the store's vulnerability to this type of loss. For example:

- Assign an experienced and trustworthy employee to handle all deliveries to your store.
- Count all incoming boxes and cartons, and frequently perform random spot checks of the contents for extra verification and to prevent bill padding.
- Do not leave merchandise unattended on receiving docks.
- Do not allow vendors to enter a stockroom unaccompanied.
- Make accurate counts of cartons containing "returns," and frequently look inside them to check for concealed merchandise.

- Pay special attention to any boxes or cartons the vendor removes from the store. This is a very common method of collusion, to steal and then split the merchandise between "partners."
- When possible, discourage potential collusion by rotating the duties of store personnel assigned to vendor check-in.
- Watch any employee who seems to spend inordinate amounts of time outside at a vendor's truck, especially if the receiving area is somewhat secluded or located near the employee parking lot. Payoffs, in the form of a case or two of merchandise in return for allowing the vendor to make a "short" shipment or engage in bill padding, are frequently made to dishonest employees in this manner, *especially during busy holiday shopping periods.*

Warehouse Controls

Although technically related to merchandise controls, warehousing (receiving, shipping, and transporting) operations are of special concern and warrant independent treatment. If your business is large or is part of a chain-store operation receiving stock from a central warehouse, or if you have separate, dedicated shipping and receiving departments, you face major loss potential that requires careful monitoring. Unless closely monitored, your warehousing departments can become cancerous and, in time, destroy your entire operation. No business can long exist if more merchandise is being stolen out the back door by employees than is being carried out the front door by customers.

Thefts in this category are almost always collusive, and frequently they are "crossover" thefts involving nonemployees. Because they usually also involve employee dishonesty, we'll treat the overall subject as an internal loss prevention issue. Emphasis is on the larger, central-warehouse operations used by multiunit businesses, but the vulnerabilities and corresponding loss prevention controls may be applied to smaller, independent businesses as well. For example, many retailers who sell large, bulky items—appliances, lawn and garden equipment, hardware, and so on—often maintain satellite warehouses and separate shipping and transportation systems to make deliveries to customers. Every operation that handles the merchandise in any way is susceptible to major theft.

From a loss prevention standpoint, warehouse operations are essentially inventory operations. A certain amount of merchandise is received, stored, or warehoused, and then shipped out at a later date. A record is maintained of everything that comes in, and a record is maintained of everything that goes out. Sounds simple enough, right?

Wrong! Maintaining control over warehouse merchandise is exceptionally difficult. Warehouses are typically at least somewhat chaotic. They are large, noisy buildings that house a constant stream of individuals operating forklifts, carts, and motorized pallets as they move case after case of merchandise from one place to another. Some of it comes in, some goes out, and a lot of it just seems to go around and around on the tow cart and conveyor systems forever. There are hiding places galore.

Often, the loading docks are just as busy and noisy as the warehouse itself. With several trucks all being off-loaded or loaded at the same time, often with noncompany drivers all clamoring for attention and priority handling, supervisors are hard put to maintain order, let alone watch for theft. As difficult as it may be, warehouse operations must be controlled, and a few key procedures, rigidly enforced, can make a world of difference. Consider the following:

- Install bright lighting both inside and outside the warehouse, with special attention to the loading dock area. Use nonbreakable light fixtures, or protect them with screening to prevent them from being broken out by rocks or pellet guns.
- Install alarm systems. In addition to your primary off-hours alarm system, install secondary open-hours alarm systems on all remote fire, emergency, and other access doors.
- Securely lock all windows that do not have to be opened. Protect them and all other openings, such as vents, with steel bars and heavy-gauge wire screening.
- Install a closed-circuit television monitoring system. Provide overlapping coverage for the loading dock area and for areas where high-value merchandise is stored.
- Install convex mirrors both for safety purposes and to aid in monitoring employee and nonemployee actions. Again, emphasize the loading dock area.
- Make sure the loading dock is well lighted. When possible, install lights, cameras, and mirrors in positions that will enable supervisors to see into the interior of trucks as they are being loaded or unloaded. Mobile lighting systems that can be moved from dock to dock as needed work very well. These installations will effectively deter a lot of the box or case break-ins and thefts of merchandise from these locations.
- Do not allow employees to park their personal vehicles near the loading docks.
- Control the hours when the doors to the loading docks are open. Do not open them before normal work hours, and close them if there is a shutdown during lunch breaks.
- Stagger break periods so some employees are on hand at all times. If that is not possible, do not allow merchandise to be left unattended on the dock during break and lunch periods.

- Discourage close association between truck drivers and loaders. Segregate the drivers' waiting area from the employees' break area. When possible, separate the receiving docks from the shipping docks.
- Do not allow truck drivers, especially noncompany drivers, to roam around the warehouse. Have a strict written—and posted—policy regarding this prohibition, and make it known to all incoming drivers. Don't be shy about complaining to a driver's company supervisor if he or she repeatedly ignores your rules.

Receiving Operations

Where merchandise is received is where the accountability for it begins. All too often, unfortunately, this is also where it ends. *Accurate records for the types and amounts of merchandise received are an absolute must.* Inventories are impossible without this information. You will never be able to detect shortages unless you know what you are supposed to have on hand. Whether you own a warehouse operation or an individual store, you must have effective control of your receiving department. The following points are offered to include in company policies, although, again, not all of them will apply to all retail environments:

- Accept deliveries only on certain days and at specified times.
- Configure the docking bays so that trucks back up flush with the dock and warehouse wall, leaving no room for cases of merchandise to be dropped off, under, or around the side of a truck.
- Accurately count incoming merchandise.
- Spot-check cartons to detect thefts by drivers and off-loaders.
- Supervisors should conduct occasional spot checks of incoming merchandise to ensure the delivery driver and receiving clerk are not engaged in collusive "short-counting."
- Instruct receiving clerks to inspect the accuracy and quality of the order, including whether an inferior product may have been substituted.
- Develop procedures for handling over-shipments. If there is no formal procedure, it will be easy for the receiving clerk to simply steal the merchandise or have it taken off the property by a cooperative truck driver.
- Consider the occasional use of a **blind receiving system**. Normally, when merchandise is shipped, the sending firm will forward two or more copies of the purchase order and the shipping invoice to the receiving warehouse office or store. These documents will usually reflect the case count and number of items shipped and will be used by the receiving clerk to "check off" the shipment as it is received. In a blind system, the identity of the items is noted but the case count and numbers of items to be received are not divulged. The receiving clerk is then forced to make an accurate count

of the merchandise as it is received. This count is compared with the documents in the possession of the warehouse supervisor or store owner, which indicate the actual quantities shipped. Significant discrepancies call for an immediate investigation.

- Test the integrity of your system, and your employees' responsibility to report discrepancies, by deliberately "shorting" a shipment, or by sending too much merchandise—particularly between company locations. See what they do about it.
- Watch for dishonest drivers who surreptitiously reload merchandise onto a truck after it has been counted and checked off by the receiving clerk.
- Make a note of a driver who has a couple of cases of merchandise in the cab of the truck. It may be an indication that he or she has detected a sloppy receiving operation and uses that fact to "skim" goods once in a while. If you can, check out the merchandise and see if there's a label on it designating a final destination; in split shipments, with part of the load destined for another company, you may have detected a driver theft operation. A call to the trucking company headquarters may be warranted, and appreciated.
- Do not neglect to count returns of merchandise received from another store in your own chain. Thefts can occur on both ends of the operation, at the warehouse and at the store. If it becomes known that accurate counts of returns are not being made, dishonest warehouse employees may simply take the merchandise, assuming that the shortage will probably never be detected. At the store end, if word gets around that accurate counts are not being made at the warehouse, the employee shipping the merchandise can easily "short" the return and steal the rest of it.

Shipping Operations

Uncontrolled shipping operations have been the direct cause of many business bankruptcies. Almost everything mentioned in the discussion of receiving operations, especially as they pertain to loading dock controls, also applies in reverse to shipping operations. Instead of focusing on what comes in, now we direct your efforts to control what goes out.

Shipping operations present a greater risk than receiving. Why? Most receiving theft is blatant and takes place right at the off-loading dock—but shipping theft may be carefully hidden in a maze of fraudulent sales receipts, invoices, and delivery documents. Although direct thefts from shipping departments and loading docks are all too common, the most insidious and dangerous thefts occur far away from those locations. For example, a dishonest salesperson can prepare a fraudulent sales receipt for a large item, such as a refrigerator, and send it—along with the pertinent "customer" delivery data—to the shipping department. Upon receipt of the shipping order, the refrigerator is pulled from stock at the warehouse and delivered—to a friend working with the dishonest salesperson. Next week, they may get a washer and dryer.

Now imagine the losses you can suffer at the hands of organized groups of dishonest sales, shipping, warehouse, and delivery personnel, all working together. Thousands upon thousands of dollars' worth of merchandise can be stolen in very short periods of time. No business, regardless of size, can survive such onslaughts for very long.

The control of shipping operations is a major subject to address in the development of an overall loss prevention program. Procedural guidelines to monitor shipping operations are, for the most part, self-evident. The following points are offered for your consideration:

- Every document used to authorize, move, or ship merchandise should be sequentially numbered *and accounted for.*
- Additional supervisory authorization should be required for the shipment of high-value merchandise.
- Frequent spot checks of merchandise being loaded for delivery should be performed, to ensure that valid sales receipts or purchase orders exist for each item or case.
- The duties of personnel assigned to shipping duties should be rotated periodically, as much as possible, to discourage collusion.

In addition to the losses caused by fraudulent documentation and outright cargo theft, many businesses suffer from often-overlooked types of improper and illegal shipping schemes, such as:

- Misuse of company mailing facilities. If the business frequently mails packages and orders to customers, an uncontrolled or disorganized system can be misused by employees, especially during the Christmas holiday season. Besides mailing all their own personal mail and packages at company expense, dishonest workers can use the mail system to easily get stolen merchandise off the premises.
- Misuse of company postage meters and meters furnished by commercial package delivery service companies. Unless these meters are carefully controlled and locked up at the end of the business day, they could be improperly used and result in a significant business loss.

THEFT DURING TRANSPORT

The movement of cargo from one place to another happens in a wide variety of ways—by ship, freight train, airplane, truck, and so on. The most common and universal carrier is the truck, so we'll focus our attention on this method of transport.

Cargo shipments made by truck are transported in both common-carrier commercial trucks and company-owned trucks. You can exercise only a limited number of controls over common-carrier trucks, but you can implement a wide number of controls to prevent cargo losses from company vehicles.

Cargo theft from trucks generally occurs in four different places: (1) at the shipping dock, (2) at the receiving dock, (3) while loaded and parked in the warehouse yard, and (4) while in transit. The vulnerabilities and procedures to effectively control shipping and receiving operations have already been covered, so this section addresses theft prevention from trucks while they are in the warehouse yard or in transit.

Yard and Staging Area Operations

Trucks are frequently loaded in advance and then parked in warehouse yards and staging areas to await assigned drivers, who will deliver the merchandise to specific stores. Unless properly safeguarded, loaded trucks make tempting targets for thieves—a vulnerability that is significantly increased if the warehouse is not a 24-hour operation and shuts down for the night. The following recommendations should help control this problem:

- If the operation is large enough, make sure the staging area, as well as the entire warehouse complex, is well lighted and enclosed by secure, alarmed fencing.
- Use only one gate to the complex, and staff it with security guards stationed in a guardhouse equipped with communications and restroom facilities.
- Make sure one guard remains at the gate to control traffic; another should function as a roving patrol.
- Once loaded, make sure all trucks and cargo trailers are locked with high-security padlocks, the keys to which are in the possession of and controlled by the shipping department supervisor.
- As an additional precaution, park the loaded trucks with their cargo access doors flush up against walls or fences and as close to each other as possible, making it more difficult to open the doors and steal merchandise.
- If door-to-wall parking is not possible, position the vehicles so that the back end of one truck is flush against the back of another.
- If loaded trailers must be uncoupled from tractors, especially in freight yards unprotected by fencing, consider the use of kingpin locks. These locks, placed on the kingpin or fifth wheel, prevent thieves from coming in with their own tractor, hooking up the trailer, and making off with the entire load.
- Maintain strict control over truck ignition keys. Do not leave them in parked trucks, even in security-controlled yards, where they could be

stolen, copied, and returned. This type of thief will follow the truck en route to a delivery and use the copied key to steal it when the driver stops to take a break. Ignition keys should be controlled by the shipping department supervisor or, at the very least, by the security guard. They should only be released to drivers upon the presentation of valid shipping documents and company identification.

In-Transit Operations

This is the last link in the supply chain: getting the merchandise from the warehouse to the store or, in some cases, from the store to the customer. Unfortunately, it is often the weakest link in the chain. In-transit cargo theft ranges from collusive theft by dishonest shipping department personnel and drivers to the organized hijacking of fully loaded trucks. It also includes "grab-and-run" thefts from unlocked trucks, unauthorized deliveries, and direct thefts by dishonest drivers. Lately, with fuel prices skyrocketing, company credit abuse has been added to the list as drivers use their company cards to fill up personal vehicles.

It's encouraging to note that the biggest percentage of in-transit theft can be stopped before the truck ever hits the road. All truck and trailer cargo doors should be locked and sealed. The locks should be high-security padlocks that are chained to the truck, to prevent lock switching by dishonest drivers. The locking mechanism should be a combination type or a removable-core, pin tumbler key type. The driver must not be allowed access, either to the combination or the key. Predelivery procedures can be established with receiving store managers for transmitting lock combinations, or delivering the appropriate keys in sealed envelopes. With effective lock-and-key controls in place, a system can remain in effect for a month or two. The combinations or keys should then be changed, just in case.

In addition to locks, high-value cargo should be protected by seals. **Cargo seals**, also referred to as **railroad seals** (because they were first used to protect freight train cargo), are an extremely effective method of detecting unauthorized entry into padlocked areas. They have tremendous deterrent value. Available in a wide variety of metal and plastic configurations, cargo seals are fastened through the hasp along with the lock. Even if the lock itself is defeated, further entry cannot be made without breaking the seal. They will not stop a nonemployee thief from breaking both lock and seal to steal the cargo, but they are very effective in preventing theft by company drivers. To prevent unauthorized access to and switching of seals by dishonest drivers (or their shipping department cohorts), seals can be numbered and controlled in the same manner as the combinations and key to locks. Examples of some seals used for cargo transport security purposes are shown in Figure 8-1.

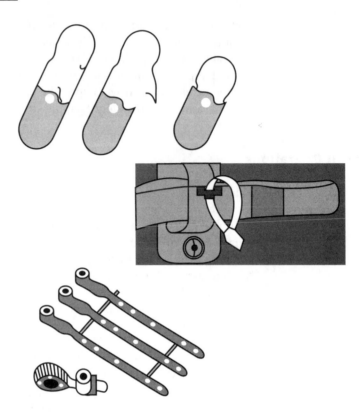

Figure 8-1 Cargo seals.

There are a few additional recommendations for securing truckloads of merchandise:

- Nonstop hauls should be made whenever possible. If drivers must lay over in freight terminals or truck stops, they should be trained about security measures necessary to protect their cargo. They should also know where to call to report problems or suspicions.
- Trucks going to the same destination should travel in convoys. The more people around, the less chance there is for thieves to ply their trade.
- When shipments are extremely valuable, consider having the truck escorted by a supervisor or security official in a trailing vehicle. The two vehicles should have visual signal systems and radio or cellular phone communication.
- If movements of very valuable merchandise are frequent, consider welding special steel boxes to the bed of one or more delivery trucks that can be locked and alarmed.
- Periodic surveillance of company trucks is strongly recommended. These observations not only divulge unauthorized stops and activities by drivers, but they also provide an opportunity to check drivers' adherence to company safe driving policies. When surveillances are discovered—and

they will be—they are of great deterrent value. Once word gets around that trucks are being followed, losses attributable to driver theft are dramatically reduced.

LEGAL ACTION AGAINST VENDORS

Yes, it happens—after carefully gathering the evidence, it becomes clear that a trusted supplier is stealing from your business. The other company may not condone or even be aware of the thefts, but they are being committed by an individual in their employ. Either way, what to do now?

In 1973, Nevada was the first state to pass so-called **civil recovery statutes**, which allow retailers to collect damages from people who steal from their stores. This means a shoplifter or dishonest supplier may be charged two or three times the amount of the actual loss. There are several legal justifications for the increased penalty, and for the store's option to press civil instead of criminal charges:

- It is yet another type of theft deterrent.
- It puts the costs of theft and security squarely on the shoulders of those who cause them, instead of forcing the store to raise prices to consumers.
- It can provide the retailer with money to enhance loss prevention programs, training, and equipment.[2]

The Loss Prevention Institute at Nebraska's Peru State College has studied retailers' legal rights in terms of going after suppliers' employees, a term known as **vicarious liability**—transferring the delivery driver's theft, for example, to his or her employer. The idea, of course, is that it's the employer's fault for not properly screening or supervising their workers, and the legal term for it is ***respondeat superior*** (Latin for "the master is responsible for the servant"). If the thieving delivery driver was an independent contractor, this would not apply. But if he or she is an actual employee of the vendor, and if you can prove the employee did something illegal (a "wrongful act that resulted in a loss or injury") while he or she was on duty, working for that employer, you may have a vicarious liability case against the vendor.[3]

At this point, you can bet that your supplier will counter that they certainly do not condone this kind of behavior and that it had nothing to do with the person's regular work duties. Sometimes the courts agree; more often, they recognize that giving a thief a job that provides him or her with an opportunity to steal from customers gives the employer at least some responsibility for restitution. One of the reasons retailers should be careful to document and immediately investigate discrepancies in receiving goods is that, when legal problems like this arise, the vendor cannot claim the retailer accepted the shipment "as is," and so has no right to complain when a shortage is discovered after the fact.

While a vicarious liability case is the most likely to result in payment of restitution, retailers can consider other charges against the perpetrator or the supplier: direct liability (also called primary liability) and negligent supervision or negligent hiring against the supplier. But all this does not resolve the ultimate questions: Overall, how valuable has this supplier been to your business? Doesn't legal action obliterate what may once have been a solid, trusting relationship? The answer to the latter question, unfortunately, is yes.

ACCOUNTING AND BOOKKEEPING THEFTS

Money represents profit or loss, success or failure. To employees, it also represents the most tempting of assets to steal and must therefore be closely monitored and controlled. It is interesting to note that, while anyone could steal from an employer, the average time on the job for workers caught embezzling—the fancy word for theft of funds—is nine years. One theory is that people who have worked for the same company for a long time decide that they are either underpaid or underappreciated (or both), making it easier to justify the theft in their own minds.[4]

The two most susceptible cash-generating and cash-handling operations when it comes to employee **embezzlement** are (1) the accounting/bookkeeping function and (2) the cash register or point-of-sale operation.

Accounting/Bookkeeping Controls

First, there is no foolproof bookkeeping system, but like the other prevention-related topics covered in this book, there are ways to minimize temptations and the opportunities for dishonesty. These include the following:

- **Separation of duties.** Unless it's the actual business owner, no one person should be in a position or have the authority to make purchases, receive merchandise, *and* pay the bills. Lack of control over all these critical functions makes embezzlement not only easy but hard to detect. As the old security axiom says: "The employee you trust the most can steal the most." At the very least, make sure that the responsibilities for receiving cash and checks, and for recording them when they are received, are divided between two people.
- **Verifications and approvals.** All accounting or bookkeeping work should be reviewed and approved by a supervisor. Invoices, receipts, and other documentation used to support journal entries must be checked. Periodically, invoices and receipts should be checked with the home offices of vendors, to verify that costs and totals listed have not been "raised" by the delivery person or the bookkeeper.

If you do not make the daily bank deposits yourself, compare the deposits made by employees with the record of cash and checks received. Make sure you get duplicate deposit slip verifications from the bank. Compare them with bookkeeper entries, and personally reconcile all bank statements.

- **Company mail.** If the store regularly receives checks and money orders by mail, consider renting a post office box rather than having all company mail come directly to the store. This system enables the business owner to control the receipt, opening, and recording of the contents.
- **Company checks.** Blank checks and check-writing machines must be safeguarded, and access to them must be closely monitored. Periodically, check the back pages of checkbooks, to ensure that no pages are missing and the numerical sequence of the checks is intact.
- **Check-signing precautions.** Never sign blank checks. Do not routinely sign checks for merchandise received or repairs ostensibly made without first examining the invoices and supporting documentation. Require outgoing checks to be signed by two individuals.
- **Payroll precautions.** Periodic cross-checks between payroll and personnel records are recommended to uncover any listing of "ghost" (fictitious) employees. Make sure the store owner has access to password-protected payroll data by computer and that only the owner is allowed to change the passwords or other access requirements.
- **Have employees bonded.** If the amount of cash or financial documentation handled by accountants or other key employees is significantly large, consider having them bonded. It might also be wise to bond other employees who handle valuable merchandise such as fine jewelry. Bonding, in and of itself, often serves as a deterrent to theft and embezzlement.

Audits

A complete financial audit at periodic intervals, performed by an outside audit firm, is strongly recommended. *Insist that the firm audits for fraud—* otherwise, the routine procedure known as an "audit" may include only account reconciliation and regulatory compliance, without the extra steps necessary to detect theft problems. How often have you read newspaper articles about major business embezzlements that had been going on for years— despite annual audits? These long-term crimes were possible because the auditors accepted at face value the documents they were reviewing.

In an **audit for fraud**, documents are examined for evidence of alterations and cross-checked with other bookkeeping accounts. Representative samplings and verifications of accounts are conducted to ensure their validity. There have been countless cases of embezzlement by innovative company accountants, bookkeepers, and, yes, even managers, who have raised the numbers on invoices or created totally fictitious suppliers and "ghost"

CHECKLIST FOR THEFT PREVENTION OFF THE SALES FLOOR

Controlling Vendor Fraud

❏ Make store management and all employees aware of the various methods vendors can use to pad bills, make "short" deliveries, and steal merchandise.

❏ Establish firm policies regarding the actions of vendors.

❏ Provide a safe way to alert store management to the possibility of illegal collusion between vendors and store employees.

❏ Rotate the store personnel assigned to check in vendors.

❏ Make frequent spot checks of both vendor deliveries and returns.

Receiving Controls

❏ Limit the hours that shipments can be received and signed for.

❏ Configure truck-docking bays so merchandise cannot be hidden during off-loading.

❏ Make accurate counts all incoming merchandise, spot-checked by supervisors.

❏ Instruct receiving clerks to check for inferior product substitutions.

❏ Develop procedures for handling over-shipments.

❏ Develop a system to account for and control returns received from other company stores.

Shipping Controls

❏ Train store managers to detect multidepartment collusion techniques that allow shipping department theft.

❏ Rotate personnel and duties occasionally to discourage collusion.

❏ Make sure every document that is used to authorize, move, or ship merchandise is sequentially numbered and accounted for.

❏ Monitor company mailing facilities to avoid misuse.

Warehouse and Transport Controls

❏ Outfit warehouse(s) with sufficient lighting.

❏ Make sure lock and alarm systems are adequate.

❏ Use convex mirrors and closed-circuit television systems.

❏ Control the activities of both employees and nonemployees.

❏ Fence, alarm, and light warehouse and other truck staging areas.

❏ Use only one gate to the complex.

❏ Hire security guards to control gate(s) and premises.

❏ Use high-security, tamperproof locks on loaded trucks, and control key access.

Continued

❑ Park loaded trucks and trailers so that doors cannot be easily opened.

❑ Use kingpin locks to prevent uncoupled trailers from being stolen.

❑ Maintain strict control over all vehicle ignition keys.

❑ Use cargo seals on tractors and trailers.

❑ Require trucks en route to the same destination to travel in convoys.

❑ Periodically inspect tractor and trailer contents.

Legal Action Against Vendors

❑ Sign invoices officially accepting incoming merchandise only after careful inspection.

❑ Gather appropriate evidence before accusing a supplier or supplier's employee.

❑ Examine the civil as well as criminal penalties for theft and liability with an attorney.

Accounting Controls

❑ Separate the duties of all accounting/bookkeeping functions.

❑ Require supervisory review and approval of all accounting/bookkeeping work.

❑ Verify bank deposits.

❑ Use a post office box for receipt of payments.

❑ Safeguard blank checks and check-writing machines; closely monitor access to them.

❑ Make sure complete audits for fraud are conducted by an outside audit firm.

❑ Require that all accountants, bookkeepers, and employees who handle valuable merchandise be bonded.

employees to cover their tracks. In an audit for fraud, auditors take a number of invoices and verify their validity with the vendors, suppliers, custodial, maintenance, and other firms and individuals named. It's expensive and time-consuming, but it is the only sure way that employee embezzlement is likely to be detected.

CHAPTER SUMMARY

Thefts can occur anywhere in the supply chain, and this chapter covered precautionary measures for a store's inventory and cash when they are in places other than on the sales floor and/or in the cash registers, respectively. Following is a summation of tips to avoid or minimize thefts:

■ **A multifaceted approach is best for theft prevention.** The store should combine its rules and regulations for receiving, inventory, and deliveries with warehouses that are well lighted and secure; inventory counts by people you trust; and vigilance for suspicious behavior. This chapter mentioned dozens of tips for thwarting the development of potentially collusive relationships. All shipping and receiving documents should be double-checked, and checked against each other, and there should be procedures for investigating discrepancies.

- **When legal action is being considered, it should be undertaken only with the relative certainty that a liability case can be made against the vendor or vendor's individual employee.** The chapter listed different types of cases and potential pitfalls for merchants.
- **In the accounting department, monetary controls are critical.** Dividing authority and responsibilities for cash, checks, and receipts is one way to guard against embezzlement. Many of the tips in this section of the chapter are financial common sense: One person should not have the ability to make purchases, receive merchandise, *and* pay the bills, for example, and all accounting and bookkeeping functions should be reviewed and approved by a supervisor. Financial audits should include checks for fraud and should be performed by a third-party accounting firm.

DISCUSSION QUESTIONS

1. Why is it difficult to control inventory in a warehouse environment? Of all the warehouse theft prevention points listed in this chapter, put them in order of the "Top Ten" you would institute, with a line or two explaining your reasoning.
2. Suggest a spot-checking system for a retail warehouse, both for incoming and outgoing merchandise—how often, how much, whose responsibility, and so on.
3. What should a store do if a lesser-quality product appears to have been shipped instead of the one ordered? What should happen to the lesser-quality product while the situation is being investigated?
4. What kinds of added precautions would you take at a retail store in November and December, when crowds are biggest, and why?
5. How would you work with the third-party trucking companies with which your store deals to ensure the trustworthiness of their drivers?
6. Do you think technology has improved the accuracy of shipping and receiving functions, or created new ways to steal merchandise?
7. How would you as a store manager work out a potential theft problem by a vendor's employee without filing a vicarious liability lawsuit?
8. What is required in your state for someone to become bonded, and what is the significance of this?

ENDNOTES

1. National Retail Security Survey, University of Florida, Gainesville, Florida, 2003.
2. "Civil Actions Against Dishonest Deliverypersons: The Vicarious Liability Issue," Loss Prevention Institute, School of Professional Studies, Peru State College, Peru, Nebraska. © Bruce M. Batterson, James E. Thomas, Sheri A. Gotrian, 2002.
3. See endnote 2.
4. Ron Scheiderer & Associates, Private Investigators, Marion, Ohio.

HIRING TRUSTWORTHY EMPLOYEES

Now that you're familiar with the many ways retail employees can steal, this chapter addresses perhaps the ultimate loss prevention policy: adopting screening and interviewing practices to avoid hiring people in the first place who might be security risks. Cautious, intelligent hiring practices include planning, writing formal policies and procedures, and constant supervisory oversight—a small price to pay for the additional peace of mind these can offer.

The size and nature of the business, as well as the overall managerial philosophy of the store owner, govern any retailer's hiring policies, but all of them have to do with a few specific topics: personnel, merchandise, financial controls, and operational controls. Specific subject areas to be covered in this chapter include the following:

- Creating a positive work environment
- Employee conduct policies
- Job application forms
- Initial interviews
- Background investigations
- New employee orientations

You will also learn how screening can improve your chances of hiring honest, trustworthy employees, and about the importance of new employee briefings to reduce the misunderstandings and other conflicts that can sour an otherwise promising employer-employee relationship. When various sources estimate that between one-third and three-quarters of employees have stolen, sabotaged, vandalized, or missed work and called in sick when they really were not, the magnitude of the phrase "It's hard to find good people anymore" becomes alarmingly clear.

CREATING A POSITIVE ATMOSPHERE

Employee problems are management problems. In other words, many dishonest employee problems are directly attributable to lax (or nonexistent) supervision and control. Policies and procedures must be developed and implemented to safeguard the store's money and inventory. At the same time, they must aid in the rapid detection of dishonest acts and the identity of the employees involved. These policies begin with effective prescreening of prospective employees and continue with appropriate control procedures that address all vulnerable facets of the store operation.

It is important to note that a retail atmosphere can be caring and friendly but still businesslike. Traits like honesty, promptness, and responsibility can be rewarded, even while one eye is on those who don't seem to reflect these values. The business climate—and the overall character of the employees—begins with you, as the store's owner or manager. If you are observed by employees taking merchandise out of the store without payment, or dipping into the cash register for a few dollars for your own wallet, you send an exceptionally bad signal. Your highly questionable activities not only foster a lack of respect but clearly indicate an absence of accountability and discipline that frequently tempts employees to do likewise.

It's your store. Control it and run it with integrity. If you don't, the odds are you won't be running it very long.

EMPLOYEE CONDUCT POLICIES

Every retailer who hires a workforce should have formal, written policies governing employee activities. The policies need not be elaborate, but they should focus on and clearly state: (1) the procedures for conducting each of the store's major operations; (2) the consequences of procedural violations; (3) a requirement that all new hires read the policies and sign a document acknowledging they understand them; and (4) a follow-up with periodic reviews of the policies.

Having preexisting guidelines and ensuring that your new hires are at least somewhat familiar with them makes problems less likely and minimizes problems that do occur. They also simplify the boundaries, so to speak, outlining the reasons for discipline and/or termination. When designing procedures and policies, consider the following checklist of control issues that might be addressed in your store:

- Establishing in clear language that the penalty for theft is termination and prosecution.
- Prohibiting falsification of time cards and attendance records, or the signing in or signing out of another employee.
- Prohibiting alcohol or drugs on company property, and outlining penalties for employees who come to work under the influence of alcohol or drugs.
- Outlining strict and specific rules about fighting, horseplay, gambling, sexual harassment, and other misconduct on company property or while representing the company offsite.
- Establishing penalties for the theft, deliberate destruction, damage, or misuse of company property or that of another employee.
- Establishing rules about hazardous work habits that could jeopardize the safety of co-workers or customers.

PREHIRE SCREENINGS

Professional companies that background-check potential employees look for a number of attitudes and behaviors, and these are gently probed by asking carefully worded questions, both on written applications and in personal interviews. The Society of Human Resource Managers has estimated that about half of all job applicants misrepresent at least some portions of their credentials.[1] So a major part of today's application process is double-checking the job hunter's data to determine whether you're hiring someone reliable, knowledgeable, and trustworthy—or someone who only claims to be.

While it is true that some prospective employees are wary of what they perceive as intrusive questions and a company's apparent "guilty-until-proven-innocent" attitude, screening can be turned into a positive for retailers if approached with some common sense and dignity. As American Investigative Services of Nashville, Tennessee, puts it: "Screening creates an atmosphere of trust between employer and employee. It demonstrates to the employees that the employer takes their safety and security seriously, especially when coupled with an overall security program. The employer provides trust and expects trust in return."[2]

The Application Form

Require all candidates for employment to complete a preprinted application form. Yes, many of them will ask to submit a résumé instead, but résumés vary drastically in form and content and may not provide what you need to know. An advantage of everyone filling out the same form is that you ask for exactly the information you want, and in the order you want it. It also puts every applicant on "equal footing"—a fancy, professionally typeset and proofread résumé does not become an unfair advantage. If you do not already have a form, you can create your own, download one from the Internet, or get standardized forms from most large stationery and office supply firms. At the very least, it should ask for the following information:

- The applicant's full name, and space to include any other names by which the applicant is known
- A chronological listing of addresses for (at least) the past five years
- Education history; names and locations of schools attended, dates of attendance, and dates and types of degrees obtained
- Employment history; names of the companies worked for, inclusive dates of employment, positions held, names and telephone numbers of immediate supervisors, and reasons for leaving
- Three business references (name, address, telephone number, and position)
- Three personal references (name, address, telephone number, and position)
- Where permitted, a space for noting any criminal convictions (not arrests).

The form should contain a statement that (1) certifies all provided information is true, (2) gives you, the employer, permission to conduct any additional credit, police, or background checks you may require, and (3) releases you from liability for any claims or events that might result as a consequence of such checks. The form should be signed and dated by the applicant. Figure 9-1 is an example of an application form.

In recent years, a number of federal and state laws have been enacted that severely limit the questions employers can ask prospective employees. Known generally as **equal employment opportunity and privacy legislation**, these laws impose strong penalties for violating prohibitions that go

FIGURE 9-1 Sample employment application.

APPLICATION FOR EMPLOYMENT

Position Applied for: _____

Name (*Last, First, Middle*): _____

Address: _____

_____

Tel. No: _____ Social Security No: _____

Are you legally eligible to work in the United States?   Yes _____ No _____

Do you have any relatives employed at this company?   Yes _____ No _____

　　If yes, state name and position: _____

Do you have any physical, mental, or medical impairment that would interfere with your ability

to perform the job for which you are applying?   Yes _____ No _____

NOTE: All prospective employees must submit proof of identity and eligibility for employment
prior to appointment. A social security card and driver's license are preferred.

RESIDENCES (*For past five years*)

From	To	Address

EDUCATION

Highest grade completed: _____

Degrees (*with dates*) or credits earned: _____

Honors/Awards: _____

From	To	School Name	Location

Special qualifications and skills: _____

_____

Continued

FIGURE 9-1 (*Continued*)

EMPLOYMENT HISTORY (*Give in chronological order beginning with current or most recent position. Include military service and volunteer experience. Additional experience may be listed by adding separate sheets or a personal résumé.*)

Employer: _____ From: _____ To: _____

Address: _____

Job Title: _____ Salary Start: _____ End _____

Supervisor: _____ Telephone No. _____

Describe Duties: _____

_____

Reason for Leaving: _____

Employer: _____ From: _____ To: _____

Address: _____

Job Title: _____ Salary Start: _____ End _____

Supervisor: _____ Telephone No. _____

Describe Duties: _____

_____

Reason for Leaving: _____

Employer: _____ From: _____ To: _____

Address: _____

Job Title: _____ Salary Start: _____ End _____

Supervisor: _____ Telephone No. _____

Describe Duties: _____

_____

Reason for Leaving: _____

Employer: _____ From: _____ To: _____

Address: _____

Job Title: _____ Salary Start: _____ End _____

Supervisor: _____ Telephone No. _____

Describe Duties: _____

_____

Reason for Leaving: _____

Continued

FIGURE 9-1 (Continued)

PROFESSIONAL REFERENCES (List three persons who are NOT related to you and who have definite knowledge of your qualifications and fitness for the position for which you are applying. Do not repeat names of supervisors given above.)

Name	Address	Phone

PERSONAL REFERENCES (List three persons who are NOT related to you who can attest to your honesty, integrity, and good character.)

Name	Address	Phone

CRIMINAL RECORD

Have you ever been convicted of any offence against the law? Include convictions by general court martial while in the military service. Omit juvenile offences and minor traffic violations.

Yes ＿＿＿＿＿ No ＿＿＿＿＿ If Yes, give date, place, charge, court, and fine or sentence.

＿＿＿＿＿＿＿＿＿＿＿＿＿＿＿＿＿＿＿＿＿＿＿＿＿＿＿＿＿＿＿＿＿

＿＿＿＿＿＿＿＿＿＿＿＿＿＿＿＿＿＿＿＿＿＿＿＿＿＿＿＿＿＿＿＿＿

＿＿＿＿＿＿＿＿＿＿＿＿＿＿＿＿＿＿＿＿＿＿＿＿＿＿＿＿＿＿＿＿＿

STATEMENT BY APPLICANT

I certify that all of the statements made in this application are true and complete to the best of my knowledge. I understand that a false or incomplete answer may be grounds for not employing me, or for dismissing me after I have begun work.

I hereby authorize you to make such inquiries of my education, employment, financial, and such other related matters as may be necessary to make an employment decision. I further release all such persons and entities from all liability that may arise as a result of responses they may provide in connection with my application.

Signature of applicant ＿＿＿＿＿＿＿＿＿＿＿＿＿＿＿＿＿＿＿ Date ＿＿＿＿＿＿＿＿＿

This application must be signed.

beyond well-known restrictions on inquiries about an applicant's gender, age, religion, and national origin, including:

- Marital status
- Family composition (yes, this means not asking about child care arrangements for working parents)
- The identities of persons who live with the applicant
- Whether the applicant rents or owns a residence
- Whether the applicant's wages have ever been garnished
- Whether the applicant has ever been arrested.

Before adopting any employment application form for your store's use, have it reviewed by an attorney who is well versed in labor relations to ensure you don't inadvertently violate any hiring laws. Bear in mind these laws relate not only to the application form but also to verbal inquiries made of an applicant during the personal interview phase of the employment process. Because employment laws change constantly, make it a point to check periodically with your attorney for new changes that may affect personnel practices.

The Initial Interview

When the applicant has completed the form, ask to see at least two pieces of identification that corroborate the personal data he or she has listed. (If it doesn't, ask why not.) Review the form before interviewing the applicant in person, and during the personal interview, have the form on hand so you can refer to it.

At first glance, look for any unexplained gaps in the applicant's residential, education, and employment histories. It may (but does not always) mean that the applicant was in prison or is attempting to hide some other unfavorable incident at a previous place of employment. Another red flag is the person who has had several jobs or residences, all for short time periods or with unclear reasons for leaving. This may indicate instability, attitude problems, poor relationships with coworkers or neighbors, or an unwillingness to accept managers' authority. Of course, don't share your "opinions" about this with the applicant—simply ask for clarification: "You seem to have done a lot of moving around; can you tell me why?" "Your application says you were at each of these jobs for less than three months. Can you explain your reasons for leaving?"

If the information appears correct and your overall assessment of the applicant's personal traits and job qualifications is favorable, your next step is to verify everything listed on the form and what was told to you during the interview. Inform the applicant of this requirement before ending the interview.

The Background Investigation

Do not, under any circumstances, hire someone without making any background checks. You may get away with it a few times if you are lucky, but eventually you will get burned. Not only may you bring a criminal into your employ—someone who finds a job specifically for the chance to embezzle funds and/or pass off merchandise to accomplices—you may also be victimized by any number of "new employee" schemes.

One of the most common involves a neat, well-dressed young man who enters your store and applies for a job in response to a "Help Wanted" sign in the window. His application looks good, and the initial interview also goes well—so well that, to fill your pressing vacancy, you offer him immediate employment. He accepts and starts to work. Several hours later, before his shift ends, he complains of illness and asks to get some medication from his car. He goes out but never returns. Thinking he may be so sick he needs assistance, you go out to check on him, only to find that he and his car are gone—along with all the money (*your* money) that was in his register, plus as much of your valuable merchandise as he could stuff into his pockets. Naturally, the information on his application was bogus. But you didn't check it, did you?

A background check should include, at a minimum, police and credit checks and contacts with the applicant's former employers. Places of residence and education should also be verified, and references should be interviewed. If you do not have the time to do this yourself, or if you feel incapable of or uncomfortable about handling the background check, hire someone to do it. If you do a lot of hiring, it might be a wise move to make background checks the specialty of one of your administrative employees, as part of their job description. There are also reputable investigative agencies that, for a fee, conduct background investigations. The caveat here is to be sure the investigative company does more than check and summarize Internet records. The Internet is an excellent source, but it's not the only place to get background-check data, and the company you choose must be meticulous about abiding by the equal employment opportunity and privacy legislation in effect in *your state.*

If you choose to conduct the background checks yourself—whether in person, by telephone, e-mail, or correspondence—pay particular attention to verifications and information received from the applicant's references. The following guidelines should help you conduct a thorough background check:

- **Talk to the applicant's former employers.** In addition to being useful sources for verifying applicant identity, work record, and residence history, contacts with former employers can provide much other useful information—but not always. Because of privacy legislation or the possibility of being sued for slander or libel, many companies now only release minimal information about former employees. However, contacting former employers is still among the best sources of useful information. If possible, talk to the applicant's former immediate supervisors. Try to ascertain character and work ethic information. Determine why the applicant left. Layoff? Firing? Resignation? Resignation in lieu of termination? Why? Get as many details as possible. One key question should always be asked, especially if the company is reluctant to offer specific details: "Would you hire (the applicant) again?"

- **Get professional references or character references.** These are not to be confused with former employers or supervisors. Professional references are sometimes coworkers, but more often are others in the business community who have knowledge of the applicant's qualifications or character—teachers, ministers, family friends, and so on. Generally, you'll find these individuals more willing to provide information about an applicant than former employers. Determine the length of time they have known the applicant and the nature of the association. Ask, specifically, whether they would recommend the applicant. In addition to work-related qualifications, you might ask about personality, residence, and prior employment history. An amazing number of people list prominent individuals as references—pillars of the community who, in fact, have never heard of the applicant. So check each reference! Job hunters who resort to such a ploy are telling you everything you need to know about their questionable integrity.

- **Check education.** Verify all attendance and degrees claimed by the applicant. If appropriate for the existing vacancy, have the applicant bring in a copy of his or her official transcript. Contacting former teachers and guidance counselors is often very productive. Again, if your applicant fudges or falsifies this information, it may indicate a reason to be concerned about the applicant's integrity.

- **Check financial status.** The best way to determine the applicant's financial history is to make an inquiry at the local credit-reporting agency. In most localities, you will need the applicant's written consent before the information is released, but this type of check is desirable because it often reflects the degree of financial pressure currently facing the applicant. Such pressure, unfortunately, is often an indicator that the applicant may be tempted in some circumstances to steal from the business. *A word of caution here: This is a specific area where you may be able to easily get information from Internet databases that nevertheless violates state or federal equal employment opportunity and privacy legislation.*

- **Ask about a criminal record.** Knowledge of whether an applicant has been convicted of a theft-related or other serious crime is a significant factor when you consider an individual for employment in your store. In some states, applicants can be asked to bring in a document from the local police department reflecting their criminal history, if any. The important thing to note here is that, oddly enough, arrests are not "fair game" in terms of background reporting. This is because, technically, an arrest is not a conviction and, therefore, does not signify guilt. Many people are arrested, but not all are found guilty of the crimes with which they have been charged. Don't confuse the two.

Restrictions on the release of criminal record information vary from jurisdiction to jurisdiction. Determine what your local rules are, and do your best to obtain the criminal history of everyone you hire.

- **Check residence history.** This is something few employers think about, but it can provide important details that either "match up" or don't—in terms of verifying data. Do the locations of residences match the locations the jobs listed by the applicant during the same time periods? Are there any residences the applicant did not list on the application? Contacts with former landlords can reveal evidence of the applicant's financial integrity. Has the applicant ever been evicted from a place of residence? If so, try to learn why. Pay attention to any gaps in the applicant's residence chronology. Where was the applicant then—in jail or prison? In a drug or alcohol rehabilitation facility? Is the applicant trying to hide something, or did he or she inadvertently omit a residence or misstate a time frame? If the pieces don't fit, you may be looking at a potentially sloppy employee—or a serious problem.

- **Verify employment history.** Be especially wary if your background check reveals that the applicant has worked at other places in addition to those listed on the application form. Why were they omitted? Is the applicant attempting to hide a termination? If possible, contact the former employer and obtain the details.

The Evaluation

When you've completed the background check process and checked the data against the information provided by the applicant, you may see patterns of significant discrepancies or obvious gaps between what's listed and what actually happened. At this point, you must decide whether to call the job hunter back in and question him or her further to resolve these outstanding issues, or simply eliminate them from consideration. If you opt for the former and can obtain sufficient information from the applicant to put your mind at ease, you should still double-check all explanations offered by the applicant that do not ring true before making a job offer to the person. Remember, discrepancies should not automatically raise a red flag, but they should always raise a yellow flag until the questions are resolved to your satisfaction.

NEW EMPLOYEE ORIENTATION

If your background checks are favorable—no major discrepancies are found and references say good things about the person—a formal employment offer should be made in writing, even for the most menial job. It should outline the person's basic duties, rate of pay, and when paychecks can be expected. If they accept and sign the offer, a new employee briefing or orientation session must be scheduled as soon as possible after the handshake that welcomes them into your employ.

In retail, it is especially common to simply pair a new employee with one who's been around for a while and say brightly, "Show 'em how we do things." While it's a nice way to meet coworkers, this is certainly not the best way to start a job. A new employee briefing does not have to be long or stilted, but it also should not be overly casual. It is your single best opportunity to impress on new employees your security and loss prevention policies, and instill in them the foundations of your **company culture**.

This is where your written policies, whether in handbook form or a separate documentary format, come into play. Ideally, you should provide each employee with a personal copy of these policies, but the important point is to have something available that each new employee can read. And remember, not all of the rules are designed to give the company an oppressive "upper hand." Some of the most critical components of written policies such as an employee handbook are the clear explanations of methods by which employees can complain if they feel they are being treated unfairly, if they're being sexually harassed, or if they witness other employees stealing or otherwise cheating the store. Written policies about sick time (and how to call in sick so that a person's shift may be adequately covered), vacation time, employee benefits, and so on are all part of a good handbook.

Go over the information section by section with the newly hired person, answering questions and thoroughly explaining any points about which they need clarification. After you and the new person are both completely satisfied that he or she understands the store's policies and procedures, ask the person to sign a separate document acknowledging this in writing. Figure 9-2 is a sample form.

Make two copies of the signed document. Give one copy to your new employee and retain the original in their personnel file. These preexisting guidelines, made known to and acknowledged in writing by employees at the time they are hired, are the ground rules for a good employment experience, as well as your own legal grounds for any subsequent termination actions if problems should arise.

FIGURE 9-2 Sample acknowledgment of company policies form.

ACKNOWLEDGMENT OF COMPANY POLICIES

I, _____, hereby acknowledge I have been informed that, as a condition of employment, I will be expected to know and abide by all company policies, rules, and procedures.

I hereby state that I have been furnished with a copy of these policies and have received clarification and explanation of all those that were not clear to me. I now fully understand and will abide by all of them.

I recognize that my failure to abide by any of these rules could result in my immediate dismissal from employment. I hereby acknowledge receipt of this document and understand that the original will be retained in my company personnel file.

_____
Signature

_____
_____
_____
Address

_____
Date

_____
Witness

_____
Position

CHAPTER SUMMARY

In this chapter we have examined how good hiring practices can reduce the chances of hiring someone at greater risk for stealing from your business, indulging in at-risk behaviors, or just plain not being a "good fit" for your store or retail chain.

- **Creating the right atmosphere includes setting a personal example with your own honest, ethical, hard-working attitude, and instilling this in your management team.** Many dishonest employee problems can be attributed to very little supervisory control on the job. It is

EMPLOYEE HIRING CHECKLIST

❑ Develop a written policy that governs the activities of employees on the job, including rules for performing each position and outlining consequences for sloppy, unethical, irresponsible, and illegal activities.

❑ Develop methods for employees to express workplace complaints and concerns without retribution.

❑ Require all applicants for employment to complete a preprinted application form.

❑ Establish a formal prehiring screening process.

❑ Subject all applicants to a background investigation; inform them of this process, and ask that they sign a consent form authorizing the background check during the initial interview.

❑ Give all new employees a formal briefing that covers all pertinent company policies and includes a copy of the employee handbook and/or procedures and policies documents.

❑ Require all new employees to sign a document acknowledging that they received the briefing and understand the company policies.

❑ Make sure store managers know how to identify a "high-risk" employee, and put this knowledge into practice.

possible to establish a caring and friendly atmosphere that is still businesslike.

- **Develop policies and procedures to safeguard store assets and more rapidly detect thefts, and make sure everyone in the company knows about them.** This chapter discussed the need for formal, written policies governing employee activities, in clear language that spells out penalties for noncompliance.

- **Use thorough job application forms.** Require all potential employees to complete a preprinted application form, and carefully check the information they put on it. Get written permission to conduct credit, police, and other background checks, and a release of liability for any claims or events that might result as a consequence.

- **In initial interviews, check identification and ask about any gaps you notice in the applicant's residential, education, and employment histories.** Clear up any discrepancies.

- **Always do background checks.** They can reduce the number of applicants who seek jobs only to embezzle funds or steal merchandise, perpetrate a "new employee" scam, or have credit histories or financial problems that make them a theft risk. Do police and credit checks. Contact applicant's former employers, places of residence and education, and references. If you can't or don't want to do the checks, hire a background-check firm that is meticulous about staying within the equal employment opportunity and privacy legislation in effect in *your state*. Based on the results of the background check, eliminate the applicant from consideration or conduct another interview to resolve outstanding issues.

- **Conduct an orientation for every new employee.** The basics are outlined in this chapter, and it should be used as a chance to make clear your security and loss prevention policies, and the basics of your company culture. Be sure new hires receive an employee handbook, and ask them to sign a separate document acknowledging that they are aware of, and understand, the store's policies, procedures, and practices.

DISCUSSION QUESTIONS

1. Using managers from your own work history, describe what they have done (or not done) to show by example their ideas about a disciplined and ethical work environment. What would *you* do as a store manager to set the tone for *your* employees?
2. Do you think employees really know their company policies and procedures? If not, what are your suggestions to change that?
3. Why should potential employers inform people they are interviewing that they will be background-checking the accuracy of the information on their job applications? Isn't that "tipping off" the applicant?
4. If an employee was honest from the first interview that he or she had spent time in prison, would you let that information color their chances?
5. Why is it critically important for you and/or your personnel department to be well acquainted with *current* state and federal equal employment opportunity and privacy legislation?
6. What is the primary pitfall of using the Internet to seek out background information on potential employees?
7. Make a list of topics you would include in a basic new employee orientation. What is the longest you would expect such a briefing to take, and how would you structure it?
8. After the orientation, what kinds of follow-up contact would you plan with a new employee—one week after hire, one month after hire, and so on?

ENDNOTES

1. "Fighting Internal Crime Before It Happens," Confidential Business Resources, Inc., Nashville, Tennessee, 1998.
2. Allen G. Lux, president, American Investigative Services, Nashville, Tennessee.

FRAUD PREVENTION
TECHNOLOGY

Thirty-three billion, six hundred thousand dollars (or if you prefer, $33,000,600,000) is a lot of money, and that's how much retail businesses lost in 2003 to sales and inventory shrinkage. This makes retail theft the largest category of larceny in the United States—bigger than home burglaries, bank robberies, and motor vehicle thefts combined.

The startling retail crime totals cited here and elsewhere in the book come from a well-respected annual study by University of Florida criminologist Richard C. Hollinger, PhD, director of the school's Security Research Project. The full results are available online (to those who agree to share their names and e-mail addresses with Dr. Hollinger) at www.crime.ufl.edu/research/srp. The study usually comes out near the end of every year for the previous year's data—2003 figures are released in November 2004, and so on.

This chapter focuses on reducing the numbers through implementation of the loss prevention policies and procedures outlined in the previous nine chapters. In this chapter, we take a look at the latest systems and gadgets designed to augment the policies and procedures, with these topics:

- Point-of-sale and video surveillance technology
- Radio frequency identification (RFID)
- Electronic article surveillance (EAS)
- Security-related building materials and equipment
- How to make prevention a priority

As you will see, there are a number of exciting developments in the world of retail crime fighting. Increasingly, retailers are sharing intelligent databases and best practices, working together in an effort to protect their assets and their customers. In other words, the thieves aren't the only ones getting smarter!

THEFT PREVENTION TECHNOLOGY

Perhaps the only good news about the $33+ billion loss figure for 2003 is that the figure actually has declined slightly every year since 2000. Experts attribute the improvement to retailers' increased use of various forms of loss prevention technology. We've mentioned a few of them in earlier chapters, but all are worth noting as possible inclusions in any store's loss prevention "action plan"—although not every system or device is right for every store.

For the most part, the technology falls into several basic categories: cash register or POS monitoring systems, camera surveillance systems (CCTV), computerized inventory systems, electronic article surveillance (EAS), and access management systems.

Point-of-Sale Technology

Today's retailer uses data from the POS terminal or cash register not only to record sales, but to track inventory. The computerized systems can be programmed to use sales data to trigger automatic reorders or restocking requests when inventories are running low. Unfortunately, all one has to do is "fail" to scan a bar code and enter it into the system to bypass the terminal. Retailers are fighting back with a combination of methods, the most effective of which is a combination of video monitoring of the cash wrap area and POS exception-reporting technology.

While exception reporting is not a perfect science, the POS terminal is programmed to recognize usage patterns and report any type of irregularity in its log of transactions—over-rings, voids, cash shortages, and so on. Over time, these can be traced to the employee using the terminal at particular times. Exception-reporting systems can even be set to alert management if the same credit card number is used twice at a terminal—once when the card is swiped in the reader and again when it is reentered by hand by a cashier or salesperson.

Fraudulent returns, which cost retailers about $13 billion a year, are being fought with computerized authorization systems that electronically capture driver's license information and access a database to validate the authenticity of the license. This "ties" the customer's driver's license number to the sale—and requires the same license be presented in order to authorize a return or process a refund. Soon, this database will be shared among retailers just like the ones now used for validating checks and authorizing credit card sales.[1]

Credit card fraud has become more troublesome with the growing popularity of online transactions, where there's no cashier at all—and no signatures or driver's licenses to double-check customers' identities and billing addresses. Online merchants have pioneered innovative transaction security systems, like PayPal and VeriSign, but these have also been the targets of online identity theft criminals.

In June 2005, Visa USA debuted its newest antifraud system known as "Advanced Authorization" to fight theft during in-store transactions. When a card is swiped through the card reader, the system instantly scans a database of credit card numbers that have been reported stolen or otherwise red-flagged (a closed account, part of a data security crash, and so forth.) Like the current authorization for the charge itself, which takes only seconds in most cases, this evaluation occurs just as quickly. The merchant can then decide whether to accept or decline the transaction.[2] There are often membership fees for merchants who want to use specialized authorization services, but most retailers find they are well worth the cost.

Surveillance Systems

The use of closed-circuit television (CCTV) systems was discussed in Chapter 3, but it is worth noting again here because of its multiple applications

PROTECTING YOUR IDENTITY FROM THIEVES

Law enforcement officials estimate 7 million to 10 million Americans each year are the victims of identity theft. In the past, institutions simply did not reveal security breaches, but a 2003 California law requires companies to disclose the failures that affect residents of that state, so we're now hearing about most of them—and it's enough to unsettle even the most cautious consumer.

WHAT ARE THIEVES LOOKING FOR?

- Credit card and **CW2 numbers** (the security code numbers on the backs of most credit cards), ATM cards, passwords, and PINs (personal identification numbers)

- Social security and driver's license numbers

- Other identifying data: date of birth, home address, phone number

- Telephone calling cards

- Home mortgage details

HOW DO THEY FIND IT?

- **Dumpster diving.** Rifling through trash bins

- **Phishing or pretexting.** Posing (by e-mail or phone) as a legitimate company that asks you to "confirm" identity data because "there's been a problem with your account" or "we're updating our records."

- **Shoulder surfing.** Hanging around ATM machines (sometimes with binoculars) to surreptitiously note PINs

- **Social engineering.** Posing as a landlord, bank officer, or employer to access information

- **Mail theft.** New credit cards and preapproved credit offers, tax information, insurance and investment statements (not including checks for check washing)

- **Retail theft.** Stealing files; hacking into databases; bribing employees of retail stores and medical offices

WHAT DO THEY DO WITH IT?

(The percentages indicate the numbers of complaints received by the U.S. Federal Trade Commission. They add up to more than 100 percent because some complainants report their personal information has been used to commit more than one type of fraud.)

- **Credit card fraud (28 percent).** Today's thieves are more likely to get a new credit card with your name on it than to charge on your existing account.

- **"Other" thefts (22 percent).** Insurance and securities fraud, health care, and bankruptcy schemes.

Continued

- **Phone or utilities fraud (19 percent).** Mostly opening new telephone accounts.

- **Bank fraud (18 percent).** Taking money out of existing accounts is more common than opening a new account. The fastest-growing problem is fraudulent online transfers between accounts.

- **Employment fraud (13 percent).** Using a stolen name and identity to get a job.

- **Government fraud (8 percent).** This category includes any type of fraudulent government-issued document (social security cards, driver's licenses), as well as stealing benefits and committing tax fraud.

- **Attempted ID theft (6 percent).** A few people are lucky enough to catch the criminals in the act and report it.

- **Loan fraud (5 percent).** Using bogus information to get a loan (business, personal, student, auto purchase) or sign a lease or mortgage.

Source: Andrew Romano, "Identity Crisis," *Newsweek,* July 4, 2005. Information compiled from records of the U.S. Federal Trade Commission, the Privacy Rights Clearinghouse, and Consumer Sentinel.

in retail. Today's small, sophisticated digital cameras not only thwart shoplifters—they are used to track employees and individual sales transactions, to monitor shipping and receiving areas, to defend the store against liability (slip-and-fall) claims, and to help patrol the premises, including parking garages, entrances, and alleyways. Savvy retailers also know that most shoplifters are repeat offenders, frequenting stores with which they are familiar and, inadvertently, making themselves known on video.

The CCTV systems are connected to computer networks that allow retailers to access stored or real-time video to investigate specific events. They can be connected to alarm systems or POS terminals, with the ability to page a store's owner or manager in case of a discrepancy. The digital images can now be stored on computer instead of videotape, and investigators can use them to pinpoint changes over a certain time period, with the ability to scan multiple images and detect these changes (and what caused them) quickly.

If a store is going to have a video system, however, it is important that only a trusted member of the management team or security staff has access to it. Someone must be given the proper training and responsibility for labeling, filing, and handling the images as potential evidence.

It is perhaps an ironic note that security companies sell almost as many fake cameras as they do real ones. Stores that cannot afford full-fledged security systems augment their real cameras with look-alikes. The experts' advice here is that if the camera doesn't look convincing, don't use it.

Computerized Inventory Management

Radio frequency identification (RFID) is an electronic means to identify and track mechandise by tagging it with a tiny, disposable electronic device that can be attached to or imbedded in a product (or case of products, or a full pallet of cases). The tiny transponder is a circuit that receives and responds to radio frequency queries from an RFID transceiver. The advantage of RFID technology is that the transponder is capable of holding much more information than can be captured in a Universal Product Code (UPC), what we commonly call a bar code.

RFID has been used commercially since the 1990s—in ski passes, watches, subway tickets, and freeway "fast-track" toll systems, to name a few—but is quickly gaining popularity in retail and wholesale commerce. Wal-Mart led the way, using RFID in its huge distribution centers and requiring major vendors to adopt the technology as well. RFID has shown great promise for more accurate tracking of inventory, particularly at the warehouse and pallet level. It gives warehouse employees the ability to check in items electronically at receiving, do exact item counts without having to open cases or boxes, and quickly locate stored items in large warehouses and distribution centers for faster picking. For shipments from overseas vendors or in transit by truck, RFID is sometimes paired with Global Positioning System (GPS) technology to enable retailers to pinpoint the location of a container of merchandise, anywhere on the planet.

Overall, RFID allows better monitoring of product in the supply chain, which results in more effective surveillance to prevent thefts or other losses. Disadvantages so far include reports of somewhat unreliable hardware performance, higher costs than traditional inventory accounting methods, and concerns among privacy advocates and consumer groups that RFID could be used to track individual behavior by monitoring products and their location and use after purchase. (Proponents of RFID say the tags are automatically deactivated after purchase, and that the transponder's signal is so weak, it could not be tracked that far from the transceiver.)

Whether or not RFID technology is a good fit for smaller retailers right now, know that it is the wave of the future for inventory control and that smart managers should at least begin to research its pros and cons. Midyear in 2005, the nonprofit trade association for RFID education—called the International Radio Frequency Identification Business Association (RFIDba)—announced a major study of current business knowledge, work processes, and job skills as a first step in creating a global RFID Certification Program.

Electronic Article Surveillance

Abbreviated **EAS**, electronic article surveillance is another, less sophisticated form of RFID, a combination small electronic circuit and antenna. In this case, the circuit is embedded in an antishoplifting label or tag attached to merchandise, and the antennas are on the poles or pedestal-style detection devices that now flank the doors of most sizable retail establishments—the ones that sound an alarm if you walk through them with a tag that hasn't been deactivated.

EAS systems include several necessary components: the tags or labels, a **detacher** or **releaser** (if it's a tag that can be removed or reused, like those bulky plastic ones found on clothing, which are nicknamed **alligators**) or deactivator (for paper tags, usually made to look like simple price tags or bar codes); and a pair of entrance/exit door **detection poles**—one that contains a transmitter antenna, the other a receiver antenna. Together, they trigger the alarm when the transmitter detects an active tag and sends a signal to the receiver. As an added precaution, some stores use **benefit denial tags**, an interesting term for an alligator that contains ink. When it is finally removed with some difficulty, usually from a garment, it spews ink all over the tagged item, "denying the benefit" of its use to the thief. And the term **source tagging** simply means the EAS label was affixed by the product's manufacturer or packager rather than the retailer.

There are also so-called **mono systems**, in which each pedestal contains both a transmitter and receiver, and **electromagnetic (EM) systems**. If you frequent bookstores or public libraries, you've seen the latter—a small, adhesive strip that contains a bit of iron. The iron is demagnetized at checkout by a scanner, so it doesn't set off an alarm when the item leaves the premises.[3]

Experts say EAS systems are effective simply because of the visibility of the detection devices at the door—but that doesn't mean they're appropriate for all retail applications. Does your store carry enough merchandise, or have a large enough theft problem, to justify the expenditure? The Rutgers University Crime Prevention Service suggests retailers ask themselves the following questions before making a major investment in EAS:

- Do I have a way of ensuring that someone exiting the store will be caught if he or she sets off the detector?
- Do I want to expose my staff to possible physical harm and/or legal liability if they try to catch the people who set off the detector?
- Can the merchandise that is most frequently shoplifted be easily tagged?
- Is it worth putting tags on things that might often be shoplifted but are inexpensive?[4]

Access Management Systems

Controlling access to retail stockrooms and warehouses has long been a matter of having employees punch in a password or code number on a keypad or unlock doors with limited-access keys, but it can also be accomplished using RFID technology. An employee identification card, for example, can be loaded with the cardholder's photo, fingerprints, name, job title, employee ID number, and so on, which is read by a scanning device. Today's "smart cards" and name badges use **biometrics**, the science that allows employers to identify workers by scanning and matching their fingerprints or eyes to a secure database.

Access management is no longer a function of opening doors to the right people. A system can be computerized to trigger surveillance cameras whenever the door is used, or to record the in and out times of the card or badge holders.

SECURITY AS A SALES BENEFIT

In Chapter 9, the point was made that preemployment screening might be a lot less intimidating if the person doing the interviewing presented the store's case in a more positive manner—that screening is a safety precaution and trust-builder—rather than an intrusive but necessary prehiring hassle. In similar fashion, increased security could also be used to ease customers' minds. The article from *Chain Store Age* magazine ("Designing Safer Stores") on page 191, presents a different viewpoint on store security and also introduces the newest technology in building design and construction for safety and anti-terrorism purposes. It first appeared in the March 2004 issue and is used with the permission of the publisher, Lebhar-Friedman, Inc. of New York City.

MAKING PREVENTION A PRIORITY

Retail loss prevention consultant Liz Martinez, who teaches at Interboro Institute in New York City, cites the "Rule of 33" in determining how big a problem theft is in a store: If an item that retails for $100 is stolen, the store will need to sell 33 more of them to recoup the loss. This is based on a $3 net profit for the item, after subtracting all related costs, from taxes and rent to security costs. Even if the markup is higher for a particular item, and the store has to sell only 13 or 23 of them to make up the loss, it still should emphasize the importance of making theft prevention a top priority.[5]

Implementing all the security and safety ideas in this book may seem to be a daunting, time-consuming—and let's not forget expensive—task, but it doesn't have to be any of those things. Many of the suggestions can be put

DESIGNING SAFER STORES

Are retailers falling down on the job when it comes to protecting their employees and customers? Some may not be doing all they could do to make their facilities more secure, especially in light of rising crime statistics and threats of terrorism. In a desire to reassure customers and maintain a feeling of normalcy, many retailers have responded by falling back on the same old script: surveillance cameras, foot patrols, stricter parking regulations and the like. But in today's environment, the standard way of doing business—or, in this case, protecting stores—may not be good enough.

Despite the proven vulnerability of commercial facilities to criminal and terrorism activity, intensification of security measures within retail stores in the United States appears to be minimal. Many U.S. retailers have been reluctant to emphasize greater security out of fear they will end up making customers feel more vulnerable and uncomfortable. In fact, the opposite may be true. Evidence from overseas indicates that customers tend to gravitate to places where they feel more secure. This fact suggests that incorporation of greater security actually could serve to enhance business profits, and actually can be promoted as a value-added business attribute, one that ultimately increases customer patronage.

Retailers' hesitance to implement more proactive security measures also may be driven by concerns about store ambience and access issues. Such concerns, however, are misplaced. Enhanced security in commercial environments need not be inconvenient, unattractive nor undermine customer patronage. On the contrary, many security methods and devices are not only unobtrusive but, in some cases, even decorative.

Among the cutting-edge materials [available today] is a stronger type of concrete, impregnated with stainless steel fibers, that provides increased building safety without altering the appearance of the building. In the event of an explosion, the impregnated concrete shatters less than conventional concrete and, consequently, is less likely to break from the substructure. [There are] other examples of unobtrusive materials that can improve safety and security . . . including shatter-resistant glazing on windows and glass display areas, polyurethane coating on masonry to prevent structural damage and fragmentation during a blast, and shrapnel-absorbing interior materials.

On the equipment side, mechanical smoke-intake devices, the strategic location of heating, ventilation and air conditioning [HVAC] systems to deter tampering, and **photocatalytic filters** on HVAC systems [the filters convert biological agents into carbon dioxide and water by destroying chemical bonds] may be appropriate. Equipping a large facility with wireless remote fire-detection and communication equipment also is beneficial in that if utility cables are severed, security personnel still will be able to monitor the entire situation.

New high-tech devices include a **laser spectrometer** [a small instrument that detects the presence of explosive materials or poisonous gas within a mile of a site and consequently

Continued

sounds an alarm] can be mounted unobtrusively on the outside of a shopping mall or other building. The device would not be noticeable or inconvenient to shoppers. Another possible security solution involves biometric facial-imaging software used in conjunction with surveillance cameras, with the cameras camouflaged within decorative or functional retail fixtures. Surveillance cameras that feed into a digital-based recording system are recommended as opposed to the more standard videocassette recorder, since digital storage capacity is much greater and, in an emergency, the information can be retrieved in seconds.

DESIGN SOLUTIONS

A number of conventional facility-design strategies can work to enhance safety. For example, bollards can be positioned around the perimeter of a building to reduce the chance of vehicular violence. Landscaping should maintain open sight lines above 1.5 feet and below 6.5 feet, giving visibility to clandestine activity. Back hallways, utility rooms, storage areas and other limited-access areas can be constructed of noise-deflecting materials and guarded by entry alarms to prevent undetected access by unauthorized personnel. Wider emergency stairwells also are recommended.

While terrorism insurance coverage may provide retail owners with some amount of protection [this magazine's research] suggests it is a reactive response—one that does absolutely nothing to protect the lives of employees and customers.

More attention is needed by the retail community to before-the-fact, or proactive, responses to safety and security. There are measures that can be taken to enhance security in open-access retail environments, and many of these measures are not inherently obtrusive or inconvenient.

Source: "Designing Safer Stores," reprinted by permission from *Chain Store Age*, March 2004. Copyright © Lebhar-Friedman, Inc., 425 Park Avenue, New York, 10022.

into effect simply by changing your attitude so that you pay more attention to loss prevention at all levels. Other suggestions will require careful review and budgeting, policy formulation, procedural change, and employee training.

A store owner's first step is to recognize that there is always room for improvement in this area—something that can be fine-tuned or upgraded in the current loss prevention system. Now all you have to do is figure out what it is, and then address it in the way that works best for your business and your budget.

In all likelihood, the solution is not something that can be handled in a single staff meeting, a week, or even a month. In fact, it's probably best to take it a step, or a chapter, at a time. Do it logically, in the following order:

- **Identify the problems and vulnerabilities of the business.** Unless you know where the leaks are in your system, you won't be able to stop them, and helping you to identify your weak spots is the first purpose of this book. Look at the store's past incident records. Ask the police for neighborhood crime trends and prevention tips. Ask employees for their opinions.

In this book, each chapter has concluded with a checklist designed to help you develop a particular phase of your loss prevention program. Make copies of these checklists, and take them on a walk around the store. Use them as handy references to spur your thinking. Don't get discouraged if the "to do" list keeps getting longer; recognize it as evidence of your thorough, honest analysis. Besides, think how good it will feel as you check off each problem on that long list!

- **Decide what corrective actions are necessary to correct each problem.** After the assessment of what needs to be done, the next question is "How should we accomplish this?" The answer depends on the problem—and most, fortunately, are going to be self-evident. If it's a physical security problem, you may need to upgrade the building's locks and alarm systems. If it's an internal theft problem, new and stricter policies will have to be written and, in many cases, forms and procedures developed. A specific list of steps, with an estimate of time and money for each, will have to be factored into the decision-making process.

- **Develop the necessary procedures and controls.** This is, by its very nature, a thought-provoking and time-consuming process, but it can be fascinating and rewarding, as it forces you to look closely at the way you conduct your business and to see things in a way you haven't seen them before.

  For example, you'll need to think like a burglar, robber, or dishonest employee and ask yourself, "How can I beat this system?" Every time you come up with a way to do so, you'll be challenged to develop a control procedure that eliminates or reduces the vulnerability. This will be particularly true in the development of your internal control policies. Start with the development of your general company rules and regulations, then work your way through every operational facet of the business.

- **Train and include your employees.** Unless you have a well-trained and motivated workforce, your business will flounder; in fact, it could very well sink. Hundreds of books have been written on training employees—get and review some of them. The time spent will be well worth the investment.

  For larger companies, and as an alternative to learning the information and training your employees yourself, the best choice may be to hire professional retail loss prevention consultants. An outside specialist generally makes a good impression on employees for three reasons: (1) they provide graphic evidence that the store owner is serious about loss prevention; (2) they can raise touchy subjects like employee theft as an impartial expert, taking some of the heat off of you; and (3) they can field questions and provide guidance about loss prevention that are usually beyond the experience of most store managers. Consultants can also be valuable for conducting overall security and loss prevention evaluations of individual stores and for providing in-depth loss prevention training for supervisory personnel.

■ **Keep the employees "in the loop."** Regardless of how you conduct the actual training, as you initiate the planning and development of your loss prevention program, let your employees know what's going on. Bring them into the process at an early stage. If you feel significant changes will be required, or even if you just want to put increased emphasis on security and loss prevention issues, meeting with your entire workforce is strongly recommended. You must help them to understand your motivation and enlist their cooperation. This is especially important when the subject of internal controls is addressed. Let them take part in and contribute to the process.

Fortunately, most employees are honest, law-abiding citizens who are sincerely interested in doing a good job. Along with their concern about their job security, they also have a realistic understanding of the many difficulties and problems inherent in the successful and continued operation of a retail establishment. Most of them probably view their situations with exactly the kind of "enlightened self-interest" Alexis de Tocqueville called a "unique element of the American character": No profit, no store! No store, no job!

■ **Implement (and update) the entire plan.** Even if you are unable to accomplish each and every step in an ambitious security improvement plan (often for budgetary reasons), commit to a reasonable timeline for them. Once you are aware of a potential problem or system weakness, it is folly to do nothing and hope it is not exploited. Loss prevention is not a static pursuit—you'll find the more you know, the more you need to know—so make sure to update and revise the plan, at least on an annual basis. Some stores do it quarterly, others monthly. Large chains use risk analysis technology, computerizing their data to calculate risks and using the results to allocate their security resources. At the very least, keep up with retail security news on the Internet or subscribe to some of the excellent magazines and professional journals about loss prevention.

No matter how large or small the store, this book includes all the basics for creating or upgrading a retail loss prevention program—with one notable exception. There's no way to instill commitment into the business owner, who must have the necessary passion to get the job done. Just remember, as a retailer, a lot of people depend on you for their livelihood, not only your employees, but your own family. They rely on you for their personal safety on the job, and their financial well-being. Don't let them down. Robbers, shoplifters, embezzlers, and other criminals are stealing from their pockets as well as yours when they impact your sales figures and your gross profits.

LOSS PREVENTION PLAN CHECKLIST

Getting Started

❏ Investigate and identify the store's crime and security-related problems and vulnerabilities.

❏ Research the options for correcting these, and decide what the course of action should be, including a realistic budget and timeline for implementation.

❏ Develop the written policies, procedures, and controls. Decide how to impart the information to employees.

❏ Conduct training, or hire a retail security consultant to do so.

❏ Keep employees informed and engaged. Enlist their cooperation.

❏ Revisit the loss prevention plan regularly, and update your knowledge as necessary.

❏ Stay positive, and remember the people who are counting on you.

CHAPTER SUMMARY

This chapter summarizes the latest types of technology for fighting retail crime, especially theft. It includes discussions of the following topics:

■ **How various security measures work** (such as electronic article surveillance and security cameras), as well as state-of-the-art systems and technologies that are just catching on (like radio frequency identification and biometric identification).

■ The multiple **new ways theft can be detected at POS terminals**, to fight the growing retail problems of fraudulent returns, identity theft, and unauthorized credit card use.

■ The realities of terrorism and workplace violence, with suggestions from *Chain Store Age* magazine about **new technology and building materials** used to minimize potential damage to store facilities and maintain the basic necessities—power, communications, and so on—in case of an emergency.

■ A summary of **major steps any store owner or manager can use** to craft the information in this book into long-term, workable store security and loss prevention programs that will fit their retail environment and budget while improving profitability by reducing shrinkage.

DISCUSSION QUESTIONS

1. Research and write a short report on any one recent form of technology (of your choice) that is being touted as a way to reduce internal theft in retail stores. In your view, how effective is it?

2. A 2005 study says most identity theft does not occur online and is perpetrated by a friend or relative of the victim. Knowing this, what steps will you take personally (or recommend to others) about guarding the security of your own credit and bank information?

3. Find out more about source tagging, how it is used and why its popularity is increasing in retail.

4. There has been some concern in recent years that the EAS systems may interfere with personal medical devices, such as heart pacemakers. Is this a valid concern or an "urban myth?"

5. What kind of budget must a store have in order to install security systems? Research the costs and potential payback figures for two different types of devices.

6. What do you think about the privacy issues surrounding the use of RFID? How do you think stores should address these concerns?

7. The issues of terrorism and workplace violence introduce a whole new dimension to store security. How does the store owner's security plan change when the focus is protecting lives instead of protecting merchandise? In your view, is it possible to achieve both without looking like an armed camp instead of a retail store?

8. On the Internet, find a liability case in which a retail store has been sued by a customer for some type of security lapse or problem. Write a short description of the circumstances of the case and, if it has concluded, summarize the outcome.

ENDNOTES

1. Anne Markle, King Rogers, and Ben Guffey, "The Retail Loss Prevention Tool Bag," on www.SecurityInfoWatch.com, Cygnus Business Media, Fort Atkinson, Wisconsin, April 20, 2005.
2. "Visa Debuts Anti-Fraud Technology," *Chain Store Age*, © Lebhar-Friedman, Inc. New York, June 14, 2005.
3. "How Anti-shoplifting Devices Work," on www.howstuffworks.com, © HowStuffWorks, Inc., Atlanta, Georgia.
4. Crime Prevention Service, School of Criminal Justice, Rutgers University, Newark, New Jersey.
5. Liz Martinez, "Tis the Season for Shoplifting," on www.SecurityInfoWatch .com, Cygnus Business Media, Fort Atkinson, Wisconsin, December 20, 2004.

GLOSSARY

A

active tag An electronic antishoplifting label that can prompt an alarm if it is taken out of the store unless it is deactivated.

alligator Nickname for the bulky plastic antishoplifting tags placed on clothing.

antifraud software A computer program that automatically detects potentially fraudulent credit card transactions and flags them for additional scrutiny.

audit for fraud An audit that includes specific procedures and cross-checking to uncover bogus checks or accounts, fictitious customers, and other potentially fraudulent transactions in a company's accounting or bookkeeping department.

B

bad check A check that is refused by banks for payment, either because someone unauthorized is attempting to cash it (stolen, forged, etc.) or because the account is closed or does not have enough money in it to cover the check.

bait money Packets of paper currency with serial numbers that have been recorded for tracing, or in which explosive vials of indelible ink have been placed.

bank The standard amount of money with which a retail clerk or cashier begins his or her shift or business day in the cash register.

benefit denial tag An antishoplifting tag that contains ink so that, if removed by force, the ink ruins the merchandise, "denying its benefit" to the shoplifter.

biometrics The use of unique human traits (fingerprints, eyes, facial scans) to identify employees or authorized persons in an access management system.

blind receiving system   The use of invoices for incoming merchandise that contain the names of items but not the quantities, to discourage theft by "miscounting" in the receiving area.

booster   Nickname for a shoplifter.

booster bloomers   An undergarment tied at the bottom around each leg and worn under loose-fitting clothing to enable shoplifters to conceal merchandise.

booster coat   A coat with pockets and hooks sewn into the lining to hold and conceal merchandise.

booster box   A "dummy" box (designed to look like ordinary garment boxes or gift boxes) with a false or spring-loaded end or bottom for quickly concealing merchandise placed beneath or beside it.

break-in threats   The various means burglars use to gain entry, including drilling, kicking, shimming, jimmying, sawing, picking, and so on.

C

call-back   An after-hours phone call to a store owner or manager requesting that he or she return to the store. Most are legitimate and pertain to fires, break-ins, alarm soundings, and the like, but some are robbery setups.

central station alarm   An alarm that is silent at the premises but transmits a signal through leased telephone lines to the police or a security company's monitoring office.

cargo seal   A device used to secure merchandise in transit. Made of metal or plastic, it is fastened through the hasp of a cargo truck or container along with the lock, and must be broken to be removed, allowing tampering to be detected. Also called a *railroad seal*, since they were first used on train cars.

cash wrap   Retail term for the checkout counter area where the cash register is located.

chain of custody   Documentation of the chronological history of evidence or merchandise, used to prosecute shoplifters, burglars, and robbers.

charge-back fraud   A fraudulent procedure in which a customer receives a cash refund or a credit on his or her credit card for "lost" or "stolen" merchandise even though he or she did purchase and receive the merchandise.

check verification services   Companies that verify checks by comparing account numbers, cross-checking addresses, and accessing national lists of stolen checks and bad-check passers. Retailers purchase memberships to use these services.

check-washing   The practice of using chemicals to erase written information on a stolen check, allowing criminals to change the amount and payee's name.

civil recovery statute A law that allows a retailer to sue a thief for more than the value of the stolen merchandise, as a deterrent and to offset other security-related costs.

clean shoplifter A person who is not really a shoplifter but acts like one, behaving suspiciously, openly taking and concealing merchandise. "Clean" shoplifters may leave their goods elsewhere in the store or pass them off to an accomplice and, when confronted by store personnel, initiate high-dollar civil lawsuits for false arrest, malicious prosecution, or defamation of character.

collection status An option for dealing with bad checks returned for insufficient funds. The check is held at the issuing bank, to be paid when sufficient funds are deposited in the issuer's account.

collusive theft Merchandise stolen by two or more accomplices—employees working together, or in concert with outsiders such as vendors and trash collectors.

company culture The values, rules, and customs of an organization, as written in its documentation and taught to its employees in training and by the actions of other employees and managers.

con artist Short for "confidence artist," the criminal who preys on naive, inattentive, and untrained people by making up stories and telling convincing lies.

counterfeit currency pen A screening device for fake currency, used by marking a small line on paper money. An amber mark indicates a genuine bill; if the mark is dark, the bill is suspect.

crotch carrier A shoplifter skilled at carrying merchandise between his or her upper legs, often using slings to support heavier items.

CW2 number A number printed on the back of a credit card for additional security purposes.

cylindrical lockset The most common type of door lock, a locking mechanism inside a cylindrical chamber that is mounted on a door through a hole bored in the door. It usually has a knob or handle on each side of the door.

D

day alarm An alarm installed on an exit door that goes off when someone tries to open the door.

dead bolt The part of the locking mechanism that protrudes from the lock body. When extended (thrown), it fits into a hole cut into a metal plate (strike) attached to the door frame. When thrown, the bolt will not retract with end pressure.

detacher A device used by a retail merchant to safely remove electronic article surveillance tags (antishoplifting tags) without damaging the merchandise. Also called a *releaser*.

detection poles A pair of poles placed at either side of a store's entrance or exit to detect stolen merchandise. The poles contain a small transmitter and/or receiver that activates an alarm.

direct dial alarms An alarm that, when triggered, sends a message by telephone line to law enforcement or security monitoring companies to signal a problem (break-in, fire, robbery, etc.).

document destruction companies A company that disposes of confidential or sensitive paperwork in a secure manner that reduces a company's exposure to industrial espionage and/or liability issues.

dual-compartment safe A safe with two independently accessible, high-security compartments protected by different locks to restrict access to contents.

Dumpster diving Slang for sorting through trash to steal documents that contain identity and account information.

E

electromagnetic system (EM) An antitheft system that uses small adhesive strips containing iron placed on merchandise. The strip triggers an alarm if it is not demagnetized at the time of purchase.

electronic article surveillance (EAS) A popular type of antishoplifting system that requires tagging merchandise with tiny electronic circuits that sound an alarm when they pass between a pair of detection poles equipped with antennas. The tags must be removed or deactivated before the article can leave the store.

embezzle To steal money.

equal employment opportunity and privacy legislation The body of laws (local, state, and national) that deal with hiring fairly and with employees' personal information that may (and may not) be obtained during prehire screening.

F

fast-change artist A con artist that uses tricks, such as sleight-of-hand, to steal money.

fireproof safe No safe is completely fireproof, but this type of safe at least protects its contents for a certain time period when exposed to fire of varying temperatures. (The most common is a UL Class 350 One Hour Rating, in which paper documents will survive for one hour at temperatures up to 1,700 degrees Fahrenheit, well beyond the 20-minute, 700 degrees Fahrenheit duration/temperature of the average store fire.)

G

grand master key A key that has been designed to open multiple lock groups that have been keyed to work with it, usually limited to the possession of a store manager or owner.

H

hide-in A person who hides in a store at closing time to break out later with stolen merchandise, or who stays inside a store all night to surprise and rob an unsuspecting store owner or manager whom they have observed opening alone.

high-risk employee   A worker whose personal affairs, lifestyles, and habits make him or her susceptible to dishonesty under pressure.

high-value merchandise   Generally, jewelry, guns, precious metals, negotiable instruments (money orders, food stamps, gift certificates), expensive clothing, and so on.

hostage con   A threat that someone's friend or relative has been taken hostage and will not be released until ransom has been paid. The person being conned pays the money, only to find that the "hostages" were never in danger and had no knowledge of the con.

HVAC   Abbreviation for "heating, ventilation, and air conditioning," the term for a commercial building's climate control system. Pronounced "H-vack."

I

individual key   A key that opens only one lock, or perhaps a series of cabinets or showcase locks, located within an immediate work area.

intrusion alarm   An alarm that detects movement or body heat, used inside a building or room. Intrusion alarm types include photoelectric, passive infrared, ultrasonic, and microwave systems.

J

jimmying   An illicit entry method using a screwdriver, pry bar, or tire iron to force open a lock.

juvenile petition   A document used in some jurisdictions to file a theft, shoplifting, or related complaint against a juvenile.

K

key control   A system for keeping track of keys to ensure that they are all accounted for and/or properly distributed and retrieved as necessary.

L

laser spectrometer   An instrument that detects the presence of explosive materials or poisonous gas within a mile of a site and can be wired to sound an alarm.

latch bolt   The angled or beveled end of a lock mechanism that projects from the front of the lock. When the door is shut, the extended latch bolt slides into a hole in a metal plate (the strike) affixed to the door frame. The locking mechanism can be configured to work by turning the door knob, or by using a key or thumb latch.

lag bolt   An iron or steel bolt with a square head, a sharp-edged thread, and a sharp point, adapted for screwing into wood.

local alarm   An alarm that sounds a siren, bell, or loud horn on the premises or in the immediate vicinity of the area or merchandise being protected.

M

master key   A key that can open all lock groups within one specific department or area that have been keyed to work with it; usually held by the department manager.

money trap A cash register– or cash drawer–based alarm system that sounds when money is removed from it.

mono system An electronic article surveillance (EAS) system in which each of the entrance/exit door detection poles contains both a transmitter and receiver.

mortise lockset A locking mechanism (usually rectangular) mounted in the outside edge of a door frame. Most glass and narrow metal-framed doors contain mortise locksets.

N

nolle prosse A Latin term for the decision not to prosecute a crime suspect. Also written as *nolle prosequi* ("will proceed no further.")

O

out-of-area merchandise Items sold in the store that are found in areas of the store where they are not usually displayed. Their incorrect placement may be the result of an innocent mistake, or a sign of employees positioning the goods for later theft.

P

palming The most common shoplifting method, picking items up by hand and concealing them in sleeves, pockets, purses, shopping bags, and so on.

perimeter alarm The most common type of alarm system, it protects against unauthorized entry through the exterior shell of a building, using magnetic contact devices and magnetic foil tape affixed to all doors and windows that can be opened.

perimeter door Any door that opens to the outside.

phishing The fraudulent practice of asking credit card or bank account customers to "verify" their account information online, only to steal it.

photocatalytic filter A filter that may be used in a building's climate control (HVAC) system that can convert biological agents into carbon dioxide and water to prevent being overcome by a dangerous gas.

physical safety The protection of employees and customers from physical harm, which is the most important priority in a retail loss prevention program.

physical security The actions taken to safeguard the building, the premises, and the merchandise of a business.

picking (1) Defeating locks by using a set of thin metal rods with hooks on the ends of them, inserted as a key substitute and manipulated to align the pins in the lock cylinder. (2) The process of collecting goods in a warehouse or distribution center to fulfill an order.

pin tumbler See *tumbler*.

POS terminal Common retail term for "point-of-sale terminal," a computerized cash register.

pretexting See *phishing*.

prima facie evidence   Evidence that is sufficient to establish a fact, until or unless it is rebutted.

proximity alarm   A silent, electronic proximity or motion detection alarm that sends a signal to police or to a central monitoring station if the slightest motion or vibration to the object is sensed. Often used in museums to prevent theft.

push-button lock   A lock that requires a code or combination be entered onto a push-button pad to gain access.

R

radio frequency identification (RFID)   An electronic means to identify and track a product by tagging it with a tiny, disposable electronic device that responds to radio frequency queries from a transceiver. The tag can be loaded with much more information than paper tags or UPC bar codes.

railroad seal   See *cargo seal*.

ram raiding   The act of driving a motor vehicle through a door, wall, or window to gain access to a building.

register reading   The running total of all transactions that have occurred on a particular cash register or point-of-sale terminal. Also called a *Z reading*.

remote alarm   An alarm that is silent at its activation point and operates during business hours rather than after hours. Often installed on fire exits and exterior doors other than main entrances and exits.

respondeat superior   A Latin term that means "The master is responsible for the servant" and refers to an employer's responsibility for the conduct of his or her workers while on the job.

S

salting   Intentionally adding a little extra money to a cash register drawer or other cash fund as an "honesty check" to see whether the employee reports it or pockets it.

secondary depository   A wall safe or a beneath-the-floor safe used to secure large amounts of money or exceptional valuables. Its existence should not be mentioned to general store employees.

shim   A thin piece of metal or plastic that can slide between a door lock and door frame to defeat a latch bolt.

shimming   The act of using a shim.

short wall   A common firewall between businesses that does not fully extend to the roof line. Locations of most short walls are noted in building design plans or by local fire marshals, but some are not.

shoulder surfing   Slang for thieves who wait near (or observe from afar, with binoculars) ATM machines to steal personal identification numbers (PINs).

slide   The act of passing stolen merchandise to accomplices posing as customers by "sliding" it across the cash wrap counter without ringing it up as part of a sale.

social engineering Illegally posing as a landlord, bank officer, or employer to access personal information for identity theft.

source tagging Antitheft tags affixed by a product manufacturer or packager rather than by the retailer.

strike A metal plate fastened to a door frame; a bolt or latch projects into the strike. Also called a *strikeplate*.

strike box The housing, including the space in back of the strike, used to enclose and protect the bolt and bolt opening.

subpoena A document issued by court authority to require the attendance of a witness at a judicial proceeding.

switch mat A thin, electronically wired floor mat that triggers an alarm when stepped on. May be concealed under carpets in entryways, foyers, hallways, and on stairways.

T

tight store A retail store in which security is tight, making it difficult to shoplift.

time lock A secondary device that must be unlocked to gain entry into the store. Used to prevent internal theft by employees, especially management employees in companies with various shifts and/or different people who open and close the store.

trapping See *wire trap*.

tumbler The part of a locking mechanism inside the core. It consists of short, spring-activated rods, commonly referred to as pins or tumblers. Also called a *pin tumbler*.

V

vibration detection alarm An alarm that sends a signal to the police or to a central station if the slightest motion or vibration to an object is sensed.

vicarious liability The legal term for making an employer liable for the illegal acts committed by employees when on the job for that employer.

W

watermark A monogram, decorative device, symbol, or name (often of the paper manufacturer) incorporated into paper at the time of its manufacture. These marks may be used to trace the origin of the paper and, in the case of currency, to discourage counterfeiting.

wire trap A wire grid used to alarm ventilation ducts and other non-door openings that could be used for unauthorized access.

Z

Z reading See *register reading*.

INDEX